M000158884

What Have I Done?

What Have I Done?

Poetry and Prose

Carrie Close

WHAT HAVE I DONE?
Copyright © 2022 Carrie Close
All Rights Reserved.
Published by Unsolicited Press.
Printed in the United States of America.
First Edition.

No part of this book may be used or reproduced in any manner
whatsoever without written permission except in the case of brief
quotations embodied in critical articles or reviews. People, places,
and notions in these stories are from the author's imagination; any
resemblance is purely coincidental.

Attention schools and businesses: for discounted copies on large
orders, please contact the publisher directly.

For information contact: Unsolicited Press Portland, Oregon
www.unsolicitedpress.com orders@unsolicitedpress.com 619-354-
8005

Cover Design: Kathryn Gerhardt
Editor: Jay Kristensen Jr.
ISBN: 978-1-950730-91-9

"I did not think of my father's hair
in death, those oiled paths, I lay
along your length and did not think how he
did not love me, how he trained me not to be loved."

—Sharon Olds

for Josh

Table of Contents

Leprechaun

She was meeting her new friend Allie for a drink, hoping, if nothing else, that there would be an attractive man or two to glance at appreciatively. Instead, at the other end of the nearly vacant bar, sat a man she knew from another life—looking an awful lot like a leprechaun with his orange beard and luminous teal t-shirt.

He came over to say hello, give her a hug, ask her how she'd been. His bloodshot eyes were disconcerting.

"How old is your kid these days?" she asked.

Later, as she tried to feign interest in the words spilling from Allie's lips, she caught him staring at her from across the bar.

"What?" she mouthed back.

He shook his head. "Nothing."

The night wore on as she drank one beer, then another, the cloudy Bissell Substance making her head swirl and her vision hazy.

"Let me buy you a drink," he said. All vodka and Kahlua and ice. It was undrinkable. She asked the bartender to dump it out while he was in the restroom.

"You're hanging out with me later," he said.

"Only if you'll play for me," she replied, ordering another Substance before following the leprechaun outside for a smoke. She laughed when she saw the pack of American Spirits, remembering other nights like this one.

"I've always loved you," he said. "I did then, and I do now."

Around the corner she kissed Allie goodbye—a sloppy wet kiss on the lips that left her holding the brick wall for balance, closing her eyes while she waited for the world to right itself again. She was grateful for the chill in the air, which cooled her burning face.

Letting the leprechaun lead the way, she followed him down the darkened sidewalks. She took his hand and slipped the ring off his finger, not wanting to look at it. He led her through the unlocked doors of Merrill Hall, up the stairs to a room with rigid reception-area sofas, and a piano.

While he played, she thought of how enthralled she had been with him at sixteen, recalling the memory of curling up next to him in a sleeping bag on the porch of that camp in Industry, looking up at the stars in wonder. She marveled how five years could change everything, could make someone who was once everything to you, nothing, less than nothing. As she watched his torso hunch over the keys, his fingers working some unknown, wasted magic, he felt to her like a ghost, liable to vanish without warning. Part of her wished he would. Another part moved forward, pressed her body against his back and kissed the length of his neck, wanting to make him real.

He wanted to take her there, in the room, but she insisted they go back to her place instead. So the leprechaun drove her through deserted streets, and the night blurred by with the fast-moving light of lamp posts through the car's windows.

In the morning she found his socks on the floor, the only evidence, aside from his lingering smell, that he'd been there at all. She wasn't sure what to do with them—wash them, burn them, throw them away, or leave them untouched in the corner.

How we met

I used to lie awake in bed at night   wondering if you loved me
now I just look at pictures of your baby   you asked me why
I don't write about how we met   I should have said   baby
I wanted you   the moment I saw you   I'm always falling
in love with other people's pain   broken is the most beautiful
you'll ever be to me   I knew nothing about you
but I knew you didn't belong there   with my mother
who took too many sleeping pills   not because she wanted to die
but because she didn't want to be awake   the day I came home
from school and she collapsed at the door   her pupils the size
of pin pricks   was the day I decided I had to leave
when I came to visit her in the psych ward at St. Mary's
I was already dreaming of far off places   I wrote you a note
in French   a 14-year-old girl's idea of being romantic
and tucked it into a seat cushion   months later
while I was studying in France   you sent me a facebook message
you wanted to get to know the person who had been
a "beacon of light"   at such a dark time in your life
when I came home you served me beer that tasted like horse piss
my grandfather wouldn't let me stay the night   you told me
I was too young   there were too many years between us
my heart shattered   but there was nothing I could do
you can't make people love you   and time   that old bastard
kept slipping out from under us   one morning I woke
to find you   in my apartment in bed with my cousin

I laughed   when I found out you gave her chlamydia
I crashed a party at your place   drank too much and cried
in your arms   in front of your new girlfriend   you knocked
her up and married her   I moved on   moved away
came back   and you   baby   show up on my doorstep
drunk   in the middle of the night   asking why
I don't write about   how we met.

Thursdays Are for Therapy

Thursday, October 19th

"Good morning, Sophie," Karen says. Her blood red lips and charcoal gray skirt suit are a dramatic contrast to her creamy skin and pale blonde hair.

"Good morning, Karen," I say.

The walls of Karen's office are the color of sour milk. The room is a small rectangle on the third story of an old brick building in downtown Portland. I can see Otto's Pizza down the street, through the tall Georgian windows.

When I want to tune Karen out, I fantasize about what kind of pizza I would like to get—maybe ricotta basil, or mashed potato, bacon, scallion—but Nikki always talks me out of it.

Pizza is for fatties, stupid, she reminds me whenever I get tempted.

"You look tired. Are you feeling alright?" Karen asks, her voice laced with faux concern—or who knows, maybe it's genuine.

I had tried to pinch some color into my cheeks before leaving my apartment this morning, but my face remained stubbornly pale. I braided my muddy brown hair loosely off to the side, to feign some semblance of put-togetherness—but my eyes, dull from lack of sleep, or malnutrition maybe, always give me away.

My body could disappear in the baggy ripped jeans and oversized flannel that aren't mine. I should have changed, but I'm addicted to their smell—a faint mixture of marijuana, the vanilla bourbon flavor of his e-cigarette, and something else I can't name.

"Please, have a seat Sophie," Karen says.

This is our ritual. I linger in the doorway until Karen invites me to sit down.

Once I'm seated she starts in with a procession of "checking-in questions."

Today she starts with, "How's the new job?"

"I make overpriced coffee drinks for Barbie dolls and soccer moms," I say.

"What about your co-workers?" she asks, scratching words on her notepad.

I tug at the edge of the flannel. "What about them?"

"Are they nice? Do you get along with one another?"

I shrug. I hate every single one of those snobby little bitches, but I certainly can't tell Karen that.

Changing the subject, she asks, "So how are things with . . . it's Jonah, right?"

Acid butterflies flutter in my stomach at the mention of his name. I'm balanced on the edge of Karen's moss-green sofa. If I sit back any further, it will swallow me whole.

"Good," I say.

Nikki cackles.

Please, I think, not now, just go away.

"Just good?" Karen asks.

"Nice, it's been really nice."

God, you are so delusional, Nikki says, her voice echoing between my eardrums.

On the far wall just above Karen's head is a poster featuring a single word in large, sloping letters—breathe. I close my eyes and inhale for five seconds, then exhale for another five—like Karen taught me.

When I open them, she is smiling. "What do you like about him?" she asks.

I take a moment to consider. I could tell her about how handsome he is, how soft his lips feel when he kisses me, how everything he says sounds so smart, how he smiles at me like he thinks I'm a whole lot more special than I actually am—but I don't feel like telling Karen any of that. So, I say simply, "I like his voice."

Nikki snorts. You're pathetic. Honestly. You're out of your mind if you think he's actually interested in you.

I do my best to ignore her, and repeat my mantra; I am calm, I am composed, and I am in control.

"What kinds of things do you talk about?" Karen asks.

"Just the usual getting-to-know-you stuff," I say.

"Are you two official yet?" Her smile is too wide, too tight.

"We haven't had that conversation," I admit. "I think he just wants to keep it casual."

Jesus, you're dumb. Do I have to spell it out for you? You're just another sex toy to him. Easily disposed of. Easily replaced.

I am calm, I am composed, I am in control.

"How long have you been seeing him?"

I shrug and say, "A few weeks," like I don't know for sure, exactly—like I don't remember the precise day and time we met—twenty-two days ago on a Tuesday afternoon.

"That's long enough to ask someone about the nature of your relationship, don't you think?" She's staring at me with her large, brown doe-eyes, her eyebrows raised—as though this is a pivotal question, as though my answer will tell her something of consequence.

"I don't know. Maybe, I guess."

"I don't see how it could hurt to ask," she says.

Nikki purrs. She knows.

"Okay. I will," I say, to satisfy Karen.

She nods.

The room goes quiet. I start to fiddle with one of the buttons on Jonah's flannel.

7

"Sophie?" Karen is giving me a look that lets me know the "checking-in questions" portion of the session is over.

I press my clammy palms into my thighs, take a deep breath, and repeat my mantra once more—I am calm, I am composed, I am in control.

"I'd like to talk about your mom today," Karen says.

I dig my fingers into the flesh of my thighs through the holes in Jonah's jeans. "I wouldn't."

"We can't avoid the subject forever."

"Why not?" I say, anger blooming in red hot splotches across my face.

Karen gazes at me, her expression thoughtful.

When my resolve doesn't waver, she frowns and adds another note to her notepad. She must have an entire drawer in her filing cabinet dedicated to me by now.

For amusement I like to dictate her notes in my head as she writes. At the moment I imagine she is scrawling; patient B-37 is being particularly difficult today. Her responses are vague. Much prodding is required to extract even the smallest amount of information. She has once again refused to talk about her mother.

Karen looks up from her notes. Her expression thoughtful again, she leans forward and asks, "Have you been talking to Nikki lately?"

"No," I say, too quickly.

"Has she been talking to you?"

I look down, then away—towards the window. Menacing gray clouds are gathering. The sky, deep purple and mustard yellow around the edges, looks like an enormous bruise.

About a year ago—when I first started coming to see Karen—at the start of one session she handed me a blank sheet of paper and some drawing pencils. She asked me to draw Nikki. I wasn't sure what she was getting at, but I did it anyway.

I drew a woman with black, shoulder length hair. I made her eyes a dark, piercing brown. The kind of eyes that could see straight through you—just one glance and they would know all of your dreams and fears—one look and they would be able to divine exactly the right words to say in order to hurt you most.

When I was finished, Karen asked me if my drawing looked like anyone I knew. I hadn't made the connection before she asked, but as I looked down at the old woman I had sketched—a near perfect replica of the witch from my childhood nightmares—a tiny key turned in my mind, unlocking a door that contained all the things I'd spent years trying to forget.

I recoiled from the drawing, pushed it away from me across the table.

"No," I said. "No, no, no, no, no, no," I repeated over and over, as I rocked back and forth, my knees squeezed tightly to my chest.

Thursday, November 2nd

I walk into Karen's office with the slow, labored movements of someone trying to walk through water.

Karen glances up at me from behind her desk, and our delicate ritual skips a beat.

Instead of her usual, "Good morning, Sophie," her mouth opens into a perfect o.

I glare at her, daring her to say something.

She doesn't. Karen is well versed in the language of fucked up. My appearance, she would say, is a cry for help, or attention. To acknowledge it, is to give it power—but no. Karen sees right through me.

"Please, have a seat," she says pleasantly, recomposing her features.

I plop down on the sofa, my nose wrinkling as the ripeness of my body becomes even more pungent in the warm, stale air of Karen's office. I haven't showered in days. I dug the sweatpants and stained t-shirt I'm wearing out from under a pile of dirty laundry, mildewing on my bedroom floor.

"I missed you last week," Karen says, giving no indication that she's noticed the putrid odors emanating from my direction.

"Sorry. I wasn't feeling well."

Could you be anymore pathetic?

"No matter, you're here now."

I busy myself picking the dirt out from underneath my fingernails.

"Did you talk to Jonah?"

My hands freeze.

"Sophie?"

"Yes," I whisper.

"What'd he say?"

"He said he wasn't looking for a relationship." My throat tightens, but I continue, wanting to get it all out—as though it's poison. "I told him that was fine. I said I wasn't really looking for one either, that I liked just hanging out with him. But then he told me that it probably wasn't a good idea for us to keep seeing each other. His exact words were—I don't want you to get feelings for me that I can't reciprocate. "

"I'm so sorry, Sophie," she says, the pity plain on her face.

"Karen," I say, my voice cracking. "What's wrong with me?"

Everything's wrong with you, Nikki says matter of factly, as if it's the most obvious thing in the world.

Thursday, November 9th

"I'd like to try something new this week," Karen says, barely giving me time to situate myself on the sofa.

I stare back at her, my expression wary. I'm wearing mostly clean clothes today, and I started showering again—but only because my boss told me I had to if I wanted to keep my job.

"Aren't you at all curious?" she asks.

"Honestly?" I say.

She nods.

"No."

"Would you do me a favor and give it a try anyway?"

Even though I don't feel like I owe Karen any favors, I sigh and say, "Fine."

"Good. I want you to close your eyes. Let your mind settle. Relax your body."

I do as I'm told.

What a good little pet you are, Nikki says.

I clench my fists in my lap.

"Whatever you're feeling, just take a deep breath, and on the exhale, let it go." Karen's voice drifts across the room, transforming into a soothing lull. "When you're ready, I want you to think of a time when you were a child and your mother wasn't there for you when you needed her."

I bite my lip to stop myself from laughing bitterly.

"I realize that your mother was absent a lot during your childhood, but for the purpose of the exercise, try to pick a specific memory," she says.

Flickers of grainy memory pass through the sieve of my mind. My mom on the phone in the kitchen. The long curly cord wrapped around her bony body—still dressed in the hospital pajamas she came home in the day before. Her trembling skeletal fingers

11

clutched the telephone in my grandmother's kitchen, like a bird's talons wrapped around the body of its prey.

Little me tugging at the thin, papery fabric of her pants. Her turning away, refusing to look at me. Her voice on the phone—hoarse from years of smoking cigarettes—even more urgent, "Please," she said. "I can't do this. I can't be here."

The ambulance pulling into the driveway. Little me standing on the porch, begging her not to leave. The desperate, aching emptiness when she left anyway.

My grandmother standing on the porch next to me—her cold, dry hand clamped to the back of my neck. She watched indifferently as they took her daughter away.

I have a childhood full of memories to choose from, but this is the one I keep coming back to, the one I keep turning over in my mind—picking at like a scab from an old wound I don't know how to let heal.

"Do you have a specific memory in mind?" Karen asks. Her voice sounds strange and far away.

"Yes," I say.

"Good. For this next part of the exercise, I want you to visualize yourself, you with all of your grown-up understanding, going back in time and giving your younger self the emotional support she needs." Karen pauses, waiting, I assume, for questions or protest.

When I have none, she continues, "Take your time. Really try and picture all the details. I'll be here if you need me."

The scene effortlessly recreates itself. The dilapidated porch. The overgrown lawn. The old white house with the peeling paint and black shutters. Little me stands in the middle of it all. Chestnut brown hair cut in a short bob—wearing overalls, with a pale pink t-shirt underneath. Her feet are bare and covered in dirt, her cheeks red and wet with tears.

A portal opens in the memory, and twenty-two-year-old me steps through. I've dressed up for the occasion in a long, pale blue dress patterned with yellow lilies. My hair is curled in soft waves.

Four-year-old me looks up, startled by the sight of a stranger stepping through a sphere of swirling light.

"Wh-who are you?" she asks, her voice small and trembling.

"I'm you, all grown up," I tell her.

"Y-you are?"

I smile brightly, to ease her uncertainty. "I sure am."

"What are you doing here?" she sniffles.

"I'm here to make sure you're okay."

Fresh tears brim around the edges of her eyes. "I'm not okay. My mommy just got home from the hospital yesterday, and now she's gone again. I don't understand why she keeps leaving me."

"I know, baby girl, I know." I fight hard to keep my own tears back as I scoop her up into my arms.

She wraps herself around me without hesitation, burying her face in my chest. Her small body trembles in my arms, as she asks, voice muffled, "Doesn't she want to be with me? Doesn't she love me?"

I hold on to her tightly, as though she might vanish if I don't. "Of course, she loves you and wants to be with you. She just has a sickness in her head that makes it hard for her to be a good mother, but she does love you, very much. You know that, don't you?"

She nods slowly, as though she doesn't quite believe me. She looks toward the empty driveway for a moment. When she turns back, her eyes are wide and terrified. "Is it my fault?"

"Is what your fault?" I ask.

"That Mommy's sick."

"Of course not!" I say.

Her small body recoils from mine.

I pull her head to my chest and stroke her hair to soothe her. More softly, I add, "What would make you say that?"

13

She tilts her head to look up at me. "Sometimes when Grammy gets mad at me she says that Mommy wasn't sick before I was born, that I made her sick."

An icy chill, like the fingers of death himself, creeps up my spine.

"That's not true," I say. "Her illness has *nothing* to do with you. Do you understand?"

Her wide blue eyes look back at me, unconvinced.

"Sophie," I say, my eyes focused intensely on hers. "I need you to listen to me, okay?"

She nods, wiping the tears from her cheeks with her tiny fists.

"You have to promise me that you won't listen to a word that *witch* tells you, not now and not ever. Can you do that for me?"

Her lips curve up into a small, tentative smile. "Witch," she whispers, trying out the word.

"That's right, baby," I say. "Grammy is a witch."

"Grammy is a witch! Grammy is a witch!" she giggles as she claps her chubby little hands.

"Sophie, is everything alright?" Karen's voice breaks through the fabricated memory.

I squeeze little me to my chest—not ready to let her go—but she vanishes from my arms. The porch and the old house and the overgrown yard crumble before me. I open my eyes, blinking and disoriented as Karen's office comes into focus.

Her eyes, curious and kind, search mine. "Well?" she asks. "How do you feel?"

L'amour est aveugle

Are you still awake?   *I'm so cold. My bones*   *are so cold*
I think I'm freezing to death.   he groans and shifts across the room
Please. Come cuddle me   he sighs, but crawls into my bed
presses his stubble   like needles   into my neck
his hand rubs my cold,   naked shoulder   smells of cigarettes
You are *cold,* he says.   *I know.*   *And naked.*   *I know.*

in another country   playing   on another loop of time
a boy named Adrien   tells me   *L'amour est aveugle*
I take a drink   *fais l'autruche*   *Je ne comprend pas*
his eyes are like orbs   of bright sea.   la pauvre américaine
I reach across the table   thrust my hand   through his sternum
as though it were warm   camembert   wrap my hand
around his hot pumping mass   of a heart   and *squeeze*
until it squishes   through my fingers   like playdough
and his blood begins   from his mouth   in a perfect stream
like Lavinia   in her white dress   I look into his deadening
eyes and say *tant pis*   *you'll never know how much I could have loved*
you.   and then I let go   and his torso slumps
forward   into the bedroom   where the other boy's
stubble   presses into the tender folds   of my body

97 Golf

David had bought a forest green 1997 Volkswagen Golf off Craigslist. Marnie found it hideous, but David thought it was a gem. He wanted to teach Marnie how to drive it, but she was terrified. She didn't know how to drive a regular car, let alone a stick shift.

"It's so easy, Marnie. You'll see," David tried to reason with her.

"I told you already, I don't want to."

"What if you and the baby need to go somewhere while I'm at work? You'll have to learn how to drive eventually."

Marnie touched her belly—at 3 months she wasn't yet starting to show. "Well, eventually isn't right now."

The car had a funny smell. After more than an hour at a time of being cooped up inside it with all the windows rolled up, she would start to feel lightheaded.

She tried rolling her window up and down to air it out, but this only irritated David.

"Marnie, please. We're on the highway. You're getting dust in the car."

"I can't breathe," she moaned.

"Do you want to stop for a minute to get some air?" he asked.

"No. We just stopped. I want to get where we're going already."

"Then please stop playing with the window."

Marnie sighed and rolled it up.

Out of the corner of her eye she saw David's fingers hover over the window lock button, but he didn't press it.

Marnie had pitched a fit the last—and only—time David had locked the windows on her. They had been on a particularly long stretch through Kentucky. Marnie couldn't sleep in the car, and kept badgering him to stop, but he'd insisted on driving "just a little bit longer." So she started rolling the window up and down to annoy him. When he locked it on her, she had a real temper tantrum meltdown—the kind you would expect to see from a two-year-old, not an almost 17-year-old. It was how she and her mother communicated with one another—in vicious, blood-curdling screams. She had never talked to David that way before.

He had been different with her since that day, more careful. She worried that she had ruined it, made him realize this was all a big mistake. He should have driven her straight to the clinic and had their little parasite sucked clean out.

That's what Marnie called it sometimes, when she was angry with David, even though she was the one who had insisted on keeping it. She would rub her belly and whisper so only she could hear, "How's my little parasite doing in there?"

She had been afraid at first, that he was going to turn around and bring her back to the trailer she used to live in with her mother.

She had apologized profusely, blamed the stress and the hormones. He said it was fine, that he understood, but he hadn't touched her the same way since. If he rested a hand on her knee while they were driving in the car, it was tentative, too gentle, as though he wasn't letting its full weight rest on her—just floating it there, ready to snatch it back if she erupted again.

They were driving through the Chihuahuan Desert of Western Texas now. It didn't look like what Marnie thought a desert was supposed to look like—with smooth, sloping dunes of sand as far as the eye can see. This desert was far less romantic than what Marnie had pictured in her head, with its hard, flatness, and all the ugly yellow and gray plants cropping out of the ground. It did, however, as Marnie had presumed, feel as though once you entered, you were never going to make it out alive.

Maybe that had been David's plan all along. Drive her out to the middle of nowhere and dump her body where no one would ever find it. Start his new life fresh, without any baggage from the old one dragging him down. The more Marnie thought about it, the more it made perfect sense. David could never have stayed in Ohio. Someone would have found them out eventually—with or without the baby—and she was too much of a liability to be left behind.

David squeezed her knee.

She turned her head to look at him, and he flashed her a wide smile, the way he used to, before everything got so complicated. He'd started growing a beard since they'd been on the road. He had more silver hairs than was typical for a man his age, and they glinted in the bright Texas sun.

Marnie's belly did a little flip.

"You know I love you, don't you, Marnie?" David asked.

Mangos

Body limp—

blood

splattered

all over walls

tastes like   mangos

how   badly

you wanted

what I couldn't

give to you—   moaning

into the pillow

hands on hips

mouth sucking

thoughts and fears—   expanding

standing over

your

mangled

corpse
        holding   a fork

fucking
    you

                      as if

you were still   breathing

       but—

I like this better now

                         all the smoke
             dissipated

exhale, relief   whisper
                I love you

it all floods back

       the sweet sound
             of your cries   as you
beg

297
      bloody little   holes

where the fork   punctured
        your skin

     like a mother
          to her   baby

I lean over your body
          and coo

your beautiful
                 warm

                         wet
            pussy
will dry
       up

and what use

     will you be   to me then   love

what use

     will you be   to me then?

Nesika

I had been dreading the move to Nesika for weeks. My mother had tried to convince me that it was a charming little town with lots of character. *You'll love it,* she said. *You'll make new friends,* she said. I told her she was biased because she grew up there, that if she weren't uprooting me from my life, I wouldn't need to make new friends.

She tried telling me the reason we were coming here was to be closer to her mother, whose health was failing. But I know that was only part of the reason. She and my father have been having problems for years now, and I suspect she was only using her mother as an excuse to get away.

I had begged my parents to let me stay in Portland, but they had point-blank refused. "We're selling the house, and your father is getting an apartment. There wouldn't be room for you, and besides, you'd be left alone, unsupervised, while he goes away on those long business trips of his," my mother had said.

I got the feeling my father didn't really want me to stay with him, either. He probably figured it would make bringing home random women to fuck more awkward if his teenage son was there.

So here I am, banished to the "charming" little town of Nesika. We have only been here for two days and I am already bored out of my mind. My mother, sick of me pacing around the house "moaning and groaning," insisted I go into town this afternoon and get some of that "fresh rural air." I had protested, but it was no use.

I was determined to remain despondent, but once I was on my bicycle, out of the stale air of the house and free from my mother's constant nagging, my mood improved considerably.

The town of Nesika, I soon discovered, has very little in the way of a downtown. It took me fifteen minutes to get there, and I had seen everything there was to see in less than five. A coffee shop, a bakery, a bookstore, a public library, a yarn shop, a cooking and baking supply store—God, the population of this town must be decrepit—a barber shop, and a thrift store.

I ride around aimlessly in loops for what feels like an eternity. I check my phone. I've only been gone a half hour. It's still too early to go home and hide away in my room for the rest of the evening. My mother will want help unpacking things if I go back now. She will give me some wretched, menial task to do, like alphabetizing her teaching books, or taping the windows and ceiling in the sunroom so she can repaint, because the current color just won't do.

I finally decide to check out the coffee shop. I have yet to form a full-on caffeine addiction, but it's never too late to start, and I have a good feeling I'm going to need some kind of constant stimulation to get me through my days here.

The sign above the door to the coffee shop reads: Maggie's Coffee House. I open the door and the smell of freshly roasted coffee beans wafts out at me. The coffee shop is small. There are several tables scattered around, all a little too close together. I must have come at a good time, because there's only one other patron—a young woman, who looks to be in her early twenties, wearing headphones and typing away on her laptop with a look of stern concentration.

There's a woman working behind the counter, but she's turned around, making espresso. She is very slim, and her long brown hair is in a loose braid. She sways almost imperceptibly from side to side in rhythm with the music.

She turns around and jumps when she sees me standing at the counter staring at her. "I'm so sorry," she says. "I didn't hear you come in."

I mean to say something along the lines of, "No worries," but I'm caught off guard by how beautiful she is.

"I'll be with you in just a moment," she says, and comes out from behind the counter and places the steaming, cream-colored mug on the table where the young woman sits, who is still typing away furiously at her laptop.

She returns to her position behind the counter and says, "Hey there, what can I get for you?"

Her eyes are so big, and the deepest blue I'm sure I've ever seen, and my mind is a chaotic mess of synapses that refuse to fire properly.

"Maybe a coffee?" she suggests.

I clear my throat, mortified. "Yes, please."

"Hot or iced?"

I turn to look back out the windows at the front of the coffee shop, trying to remember the weather, so I can infer which would be the most appropriate option.

She laughs, and it is the sound of zephyr-blown wind chimes. "Are you waiting for someone? You seem nervous."

"No, I'm sorry. I was just . . . I'll take an iced coffee, please. With cream, no sugar."

"You got it. That'll be just a moment." She starts to turn around to make my coffee.

"Leo, my name's Leo," I say much too loudly in my panic.

"It's nice to meet you, Leo," she says, holding out her hand with a bemused expression.

I shake her small, bird-like hand, in mine, which is clammy, and grotesquely large by comparison.

"My name is Simone," she says.

Air

is *the source* from which all else comes alive
like the yeast foaming and rising and bubbling
in the warm water and molasses, that sweet
dark syrup—sticky like sex on your skin—when
the twin loaves come steaming out of the oven
you think of Christ, and say, "Take, eat; this is
my body," presenting the bread, still warm from
the oven, to the apparition before you, and he takes
with his hands, and his mouth, hungry—groping
and gnawing, and it feels so good, even the guilt
to be devoured—the living yeast foaming and rising
and bubbling—Take, eat; this is my body—bubbling
in the warm, wanting only to be consumed, dripping
sweet, dark molasses, and the apparition is nearly
solid, as he tells you how good your bread tastes
and you thank him, with regret that he isn't real
that tomorrow your fingers will grope for him in
the early dawn—when the birds are singing sweetly
to one another, outside your window, through
condensation—hung in a half moon—and they
will close into fists, around nothing but air.

Like Gold in the Afternoon Sun

"Do you have to smoke inside, Mom?" Marnie asked.

Her mother was sitting on the couch—a green and yellow upholstered monstrosity they had acquired from the trailer's previous occupants—watching a soap Marnie didn't know the name of.

"You're getting ash all over the carpet."

Her mother brought the cigarette to her lips. "Aren't you going to be late for school or something?"

"Whatever," Marnie said, opening the front door and slamming it behind her.

Her best friend Tammy was already sitting in the driveway, idling her Volkswagen Rabbit.

"Fucking bitch," Marnie spat as she got in the car.

Tammy was engaged with her reflection in the driver's side mirror, applying a fresh coat of mascara. "What'd she do this time?"

"I don't want to talk about it."

Tammy shrugged, returning the mascara wand back to its bright orange tube. "Coffee?"

"Please," Marnie said, rubbing her temples. "I don't think I slept a wink last night."

As they were pulling out of the Dunkin Donuts drive-thru, Tammy said, "How come you never wear makeup?"

Marnie rolled her eyes. "Not this again."

Tammy pouted her lips in mock innocence as she fiddled with the radio. "I'm just curious, that's all."

Marnie shrugged. There was still a thick morning fog surrounding her brain. "I never learned how, I guess."

Tammy gasped in horror, swerving the Rabbit. "How is that even possible?"

"I don't know," Marnie said, rolling her eyes. "My mother doesn't love me or something, I guess?"

"Well," she said after a moment, "I'll do it for you. You'd look *so* good with some mascara, maybe a little eyeshadow . . ."

Marnie sighed. "If you can manage not to kill us on the way to school, I'll think about it."

"Oh, come on, don't be so boring," Tammy teased, reaching over to muss up Marnie's hair. "We can swing by Rite Aid after school."

"Do you have to do that? My hair looks bad enough as it is," Marnie huffed, trying to smooth it back down with her fingers. "You know I don't have money for makeup, anyway."

Tammy laughed. "Who said anything about paying for it?"

"Right. Silly me."

"I'm taking that as a yes," Tammy said, smiling as they pulled into the high school parking lot.

As the two girls walked side by side through the high school's main entrance, Marnie pouted at her reflection in the glass doors.

"Stop it, you're adorable," Tammy said, gently pinching her arm.

"Fuck," Marnie said under her breath.

"Oh, come on. I didn't pinch you that hard."

"No, not that," Marnie hissed. "Look." She pointed her chin in the direction of their English teacher, Mr. Norton.

"Oh, boy. Here we go."

"Shut up, he's coming over."

"Good morning, ladies," Mr. Norton said, beaming.

"Morning, Mr. Norton," Tammy said, her voice low, oozing something Marnie didn't quite know how to describe.

"Hey," Marnie said, just as the bell for first period rang.

"Uh oh, you ladies better be off to class," Mr. Norton said.

Marnie inhaled sharply as they walked away.

Tammy put a comforting arm around her shoulder. Marnie knew Tammy didn't get why she had the hots for Mr. Norton. Tammy thought he looked "incredibly nerdy," and that the "pedophile stash" he'd grown over the summer was "ridiculous."

"Oh, *honestly*," Tammy said as they made their way through the crowded hallways.

"He's so handsome," Marnie whispered.

"He's so *old*," Tammy said.

"Shhh, keep your voice down!" Marnie said, squeezing her arm. "He's only thirty-four, and he's a runner. So he's going to live for a long time."

"Running makes you live longer? Is that how that works?"

"Eat a dick."

"Good one, babe. Hey, do you think he wears those really short shorts when he runs?"

"I hope so," Marnie said, her cheeks coloring as she pictured Mr. Norton in running shorts.

Tammy sighed and shook her head. "This is you."

"Oh," Marnie said. She hadn't noticed they were standing in front of her first period classroom—bio with Mr. Wilson.

"You okay, ya little weirdo?" Tammy asked, nudging her playfully in the ribs.

"Yeah, I'm fine. Thanks for walking me to class."

"No problem. See you at lunch," Tammy said. Her butt cheeks bounced provocatively in her leopard print mini-skirt as she walked away.

At lunch Marnie sat next to Tammy at their usual table in the corner of the cafeteria. It gave them the best view for Tammy's favorite activity—ogling boys.

"Is Paul dreamy or what?"

Marnie was peeling the rind from an orange. Citrus sprayed across the table as she broke into the flesh with her fingernail. "He's alright."

"Oh, come on, Marnie!"

Marnie shrugged. "I'm subtracting points for his shitty personality. The guy's a douche."

Tammy crossed her arms. "His personality isn't going to matter when he's fucking you."

"Of course, it will. I want to lose my virginity to someone who is going to care whether or not I have a good time. Not someone like Paul, who is clearly incapable of thinking about anyone but himself."

Tammy threw her arms in the air. "Jesus, Marnie. Do you *ever* want to get laid?"

"Sure, eventually. What's the rush?"

"You're *fif*teen! Guys are going to think there's something wrong with you if you don't lose it soon. And then no will want to fuck you, and you'll end up alone!" Tammy said several octaves higher than she should have, attracting shocked stares from nearby tables.

"Tammy, would you keep it down?" Marnie pleaded in a furious whisper, before hiding her head in her hands.

"Is everything alright over here, girls?"

Marnie would recognize that voice anywhere. The way it dripped smooth as honey, making it difficult for her to breathe.

"Everything's just fine, Mr. Norton," Tammy said.

"Marnie?" He was leaning forward, resting his hands on his knees.

29

Marnie lifted her head sheepishly. "I'm fine." His proximity to her was making her heart flutter.

"I missed you in class yesterday. Were you not feeling well?"

Tammy had convinced her to skip last period yesterday to tan down by the river. No one was there that time of day, which meant they could tan topless. It had surprised Marnie the first time they'd done it, how good the warm sun felt on her bare breasts.

"Marnie?" Mr. Norton said.

"Sorry, yeah, I wasn't feeling well. I'm better now, though."

"I'm glad to hear that. Can you stop by my room after school today?"

"Yeah, um, sure. Okay."

Due to its location in the building, Mr. Norton's classroom was full of sun this time of day. He was sitting at his desk, typing at his computer when Marnie walked in.

"Hey there, Marnie," he said, looking at her—his eyes lit up like gold in the afternoon sun.

"Hey, Mr. Norton," she said, meeting his gaze briefly, before turning to look away, out the window at the students getting on the bus.

"Can I help you with something?" he asked, his voice again taking on that tone of dripping honey.

"You wanted to see me?"

"Yes, I did." He stood and walked around to the front of his desk as he spoke. "Why don't you have a seat?" He motioned to a desk in the front row as he leaned back on the edge of his own.

Marnie walked over to the desk, placed her backpack on the floor, and sat down. She looked up at Mr. Norton. He was staring at her with a concerned crease in his brows.

"Am I in trouble?" she asked.

Mr. Norton rubbed his chin with his thumb and forefinger. "No," he said, and then after a contemplative pause, added, "Not yet, anyway."

Marnie wiped her clammy palms on her jeans under the table.

"I've noticed that you have been spending more and more time with that Tammy girl." Marnie's mouth opened, but before she could say anything, Mr. Norton continued, "I see a lot of potential in you, Marnie. I'd hate to see you squander it."

Her brain raced as she struggled to form a coherent thought. "I'm sorry, I don't think I understand."

Mr. Norton folded his hands, placing them over his left knee. "I'll be blunt then. I'm concerned that hanging around with Tammy is having a negative impact on you. Already twice this month you've missed class, and I've begun to notice a decline in the quality of your work."

Marnie's face burned with equal amounts of embarrassment, anger, and frustration. She didn't know what to say.

Mr. Norton leaned forward. "Marnie, do you remember the poem we read last week, 'The Summer Day,' by Mary Oliver?"

Marnie shrugged. She vaguely remembered something about a grasshopper, but not much else. She'd been having trouble concentrating in class lately. There was too much else on her mind.

Mr. Norton sighed. "The last couple lines of the poem are, I believe, particularly pertinent to our current predicament. 'Tell me, what is it you plan to do, with your one wild and precious life?'"

It was coming back to Marnie now—the way Mr. Norton had looked directly at her as he had delivered those same lines to the class the week before, how it had made her squirm in her seat.

" *This* is *your* one wild and precious life, Marnie, just sitting in the palm of your hands. Don't throw it away."

Marnie stood up. Her throat was dry and tight. "I have to go."

"Please," he said, grabbing her wrist. "You're better than this."

Mr. Norton's hand was electric on her skin. She closed her eyes, and repeated, "I have to go."

31

He loosened his fingers from around her wrist and coughed, turning to look out the window.

Marnie slung her backpack over her shoulder and walked out of the room.

Her wrist was still burning from Mr. Norton's touch when she reached the parking lot.

Tammy was posed on the hood of her Rabbit, smoking a joint. Her long legs stretched out before her, soaking up the sun.

Marnie wiped at her face with the sleeve of her hoodie and opened the Rabbit's passenger door.

"What's wrong?" Tammy asked.

"Nothing. Let's go."

Tammy climbed into the driver's seat next to Marnie. "Did you get a bad grade on your paper or something?"

"I don't want to talk about it."

"Okay, sorry I asked," Tammy said, exhaling smoke into the car.

"I'm sorry. I've just had a shit day."

"No worries," Tammy said, as she pulled the Rabbit out of the high school parking lot. "Wanna smoke?"

Marnie didn't really care for pot all that much. She didn't like the way it made her brain feel fuzzy and numb, but after the encounter she'd just had with Mr. Norton, feeling fuzzy and numb sounded sublime. "Fuck it," she said. "Why not?"

Back in Tammy's room, she and Marnie sucked down their after school iced coffees while they admired the pile of makeup Tammy had emptied out onto her bed.

"Shit," Marnie said. "I didn't see you take half this stuff."

"That's because I'm sneaky," she replied with a wicked smile. "Now close your eyes."

Marnie made a face. "You promise you won't make me look stupid?"

"Promise."

Marnie closed her eyes reluctantly.

A second later, she felt Tammy's cool fingers brush across her face.

Marnie giggled.

"Shhh," Tammy said, "Don't move or you'll fuck it up."

"Sorry."

Tammy continued to brush this and dab that onto Marnie's face.

"Are you done yet?" she sighed.

"Perfection takes time. Be patient."

"I bet I look ridiculous."

"I'm just adding the final touches. Quit whining."

Marnie sighed.

After a few more minutes, which felt like an eternity to Marnie, Tammy said, "Alright, you can open your eyes now."

Marnie blinked her heavy lids open. Tammy was holding a hand mirror up in front of her face.

"Well, what do you think, babe?" Tammy asked.

Marnie was speechless. As she looked at her reflection in the mirror, she realized for the first time why girls wore makeup. She looked at least two years older, and *almost* beautiful.

"That bad, huh?"

Marnie cleared her throat. "No, not at all. I actually kind of like it. Thank you."

Tammy smiled and kissed Marnie on the cheek. "I knew you would."

On the walk home—which took less than a minute, since Marnie's trailer was only four down from Tammy's—Marnie's head buzzed from the high, and Tammy's lips, and the feel of her warm body so close to her own.

As she opened her front door the smell of cigarettes and stale air rushed out to greet her. Her mother was passed out on the couch—mouth open and crusty with drool. Greasy strands of hair clung to her sweaty face. Her bloated abdomen rose and fell with each heavy breath.

Marnie closed her eyes and imagined she was back in Mr. Norton's classroom—only this time he didn't let go of her wrist, and she didn't say she had to go.

Carcass

all these little birds keep picking at me
hard, determined beaks peck through skin, scrape
against bone—they dance and chirp ominous tones
flap their wings, rhythmically in circles like
something tribal, as I writhe, helpless as a worm
in a pool of blood—the lions come, with their heads hung
low, my blood stains their mouths purple, the color
of wine, a drunk hum, a chorus of purrs—resonates
just audible beneath the squawking of the birds

No One

Vincent

That stupid cunt. Who the fuck does she think she is? Showing up at my apartment unannounced. What did she expect to find? No matter, she'll get over it. The bitch isn't going anywhere. Sure, she'll be mad for a couple of days, but then I'll apologize, bring her flowers, pretend to show remorse, fuck her all nice and gentle the way she likes, and she'll forgive me.

Simone

Driving towards Vincent's apartment, I am so nervous I grip the steering wheel until my knuckles turn white.

I've never just shown up uninvited . . . but he hasn't picked up his phone all day. So, like the loving girlfriend that I am, I baked his favorite cookies, put them in a to-go container, and got in my car.

I knock tentatively on the door, the container of cookies shaking in my hand. When no one answers I try the knob—it's unlocked, so I let myself in.

Several things seem to happen all at once. I hear a woman moaning loudly. The container of cookies slips from my hands. It hits the floor. The glass shatters around the heap of gooey baked goods. The noise in the bedroom stops. Vincent walks out into the living room butt naked. His face turns white when he sees me.

His mouth is moving, but no sound comes out. A girl wearing nothing but one of his t-shirts runs past me out the door. I only catch a brief glimpse of her—platinum hair and long legs. *How fucking original.*

For what feels like a very long time, everything is fuzzy. My legs tingle and become Jell-O.

"It's not what it looks like, Simona." He thinks my name sounds better ending with an a, then with an e. *Simona is romantic, elegant. Simone falls flat.*

"I love you. She's no one. No one, okay?"

I slowly shake my head, my eyes welling with tears.

"Baby, please, say something."

"How could you?" My voice is weak and small.

"Baby, it's not like that. She's just some girl who followed me home from the bar. She was drunk and needed a place to stay." He sounds exasperated, like he's trying to explain something to a child.

"I could hear you fucking her . . ."

"She climbed on top of me! I was hungover and disorientated. I threw her off as soon as I realized what was happening."

"You're a real shitty liar, you know that?"

"I love you. I don't want anyone else. I made a mistake okay, baby? I'll make it up to you.   I promise." He reaches out to me, the backs of his knuckles brush down my cheek.

For a brief instant, I am somewhere else, somewhere outside of this moment.

His fingers are tracing my collar bone, he is moving closer.

I inhale deeply. The air smells faintly of perfume, lingering in the space where she had been.

"No," I say.

"Mona . . ."

"No!" I say and push him from me. "Don't touch me."

He reaches out again, and coos, "Mona, baby, please, don't be like this."

"I will scream," I say, as I back away from him. "I will scream if you touch me."

He stops.

"I'm leaving. Don't follow me." I turn my back to him and run from his apartment.

"Mona . . ."

His voice echoes and reverberates in the stairwell. *Mona mona mona* . . . It's all I hear on the drive back home, his voice calling my name—*Mona mona mona*—empty and hollow.

Vincent

Most guys would have made the mistake of running after her, but that's the worst thing you can do. The wound is too fresh. She'll say things she doesn't mean, and you might, too, because you can't help yourself. You might slip up and tell her what a stupid cunt you think she is, but this will only make things worse, so you let her leave. Let her vent to her best friend, and then later that night, cry herself to sleep.

In the dawn of a new day, her anger will settle, and things will shift into perspective. She is miserable and lonely without you— always go for the lonely ones—they're the easiest to manipulate, always so desperate for your affection—that's when you show up on her doorstep with flowers. You tell her what a stupid, stupid mistake you made. You beg her to take you back, tell her that you couldn't live without her. She is your everything. All the rest is just noise. You promise her it will never happen again, while you think to yourself that you will have to be more careful next time.

But that's tomorrow. Today, you go and fetch the slut you're cheating on your girlfriend with—the slut who thinks you will eventually leave your girlfriend for *her*—you bring her back to your place and fuck her in the ass then cum on her face, because your girlfriend finds these things degrading and won't let you do them to her.

nesting season

dark clumps of hair cling
to my mother's oily forehead

her eyes dart
side to side, like a trapped animal

Treehouse

Charles took another sip from his warm PBR, stealing a sideways glance at his best friend James, who was sitting at the other end of the brown leather, L-shaped couch—Stacey Newton giggling in his lap.

Stacey was supposed to bring a friend for Charles, but when she arrived, she claimed not one of them had wanted to come. Charles didn't believe this. She'd had it out for him since day one. He didn't think she much liked having to compete for James' attention. Well, the joke was on her, if she thought James would ever choose a bottle-blonde, braindead bimbo over his best friend.

It was only for a few more weeks, he had to keep reminding himself. Summer would be over soon, and Charles and James would be heading off to Yale, leaving this godforsaken town, and Stacey Newton—who was only a junior—behind them. Not that Charles had anything to worry about, even if Stacey were a senior, it's not like *she* would have got accepted into Yale. She'd be lucky if a community college wanted to take her. Although, if Charles were being honest, he imagined that Stacey had something much more *acrobatic*, than academic, in her future.

When Stacey started kissing James' neck, making wet, slurping noises, Charles decided he'd had enough. "I'm going for a walk," he said, pushing himself up from the deep impression he'd been wearing in James' couch.

James had the decency, at least, to mouth an, "I'm sorry," before redirecting his attention back to Stacey.

Charles took the last warm sip of his beer. It was beyond him—who in their right mind would name their sweet, innocent baby, *Stacey*? His mouth felt sticky after saying it, as though it left behind a residue he couldn't spit out.

He grabbed a couple more PBRs from the mini-fridge before exiting the basement through the sliding glass doors that let out onto the backyard patio. The warm summer air hit him in a rush. The sudden change from the cool of the basement made him dizzy, and he had to lean against the glass for a moment to let his head clear.

He cracked open one of the fresh cans of beer, and let the cold liquid pour down his throat until it was more than halfway gone. He sighed and wiped his mouth.

He was about to go back inside and tell Stacey to leave, when he caught the scent of cigarette smoke in the air. Intrigued—no one in James' family smoked—he cupped his hands around his eyes and peered into the darkness.

There, at the far end of the patio, was a small figure balled up in a lawn chair, holding a cigarette to her lips.

Charles smiled. He strode over to her with noiseless steps. "Aren't you a little young to be smoking?"

His voice made her jump.

"You must be Clara's friend, Marnie. James mentioned his sister was having a sleepover."

When she saw Charles, she relaxed, and took a long drag from her cigarette. On the exhale, through a stream of white smoke, she said, "Oh, it's just you."

Charles sat down in the chair closest to her. "Just me? You're not worried I'll tell on you?"

"No."

"Why's that?"

She turned her wide, gray-blue eyes on him. "Because then I'd have to tell James' parents that he snuck a girl into the house."

He wanted to say, *Clever little shit, aren't we?* but he bit his tongue.

"It seems we've come to an impasse."

Charles sighed, deciding to change tactics. "I'm sorry, Marnie. I was just teasing. I would never tell on you."

She continued smoking, as though he weren't there.

"Could I bum a smoke?"

She shrugged, pulling a pack of American Spirits from the pocket of her pajama shorts. She removed a single cigarette and handed it to him.

Maybe it was the heat, or the beer, but he couldn't help himself. The voice in the back of his head whispering, *she's only thirteen*, was fading by the minute.

"Want a beer?" he asked, offering her the extra can he had brought outside with him.

"Aren't I a little young to be drinking?"

He pressed his lips together to keep from laughing. "One beer won't hurt you any."

She shrugged, taking the can of beer from his outstretched hand with a degree of indifference unusual for someone of her age. "How come you're not inside hanging out with your friends?"

"How come you're not inside hanging out with Clara?"

Sighing, she replied, "Clara's sleeping."

"Well, James and Stacey are . . . I thought I'd give them some privacy."

She took an irritatingly small sip of her beer. Charles had to fight the urge to tip the can upwards.

"Why aren't *you* sleeping?" he asked.

She turned her whole body to look at him. Her eyes, reflecting the light of the moon, looked like slivers of ice. "What do you want from me?"

"Jesus, Marnie. I'm just trying to have a conversation with you. Why do you have to make it so difficult?"

"You've never tried to have a conversation with me before." Her face was all eyes, and cheekbones, and pouty lips. She was wearing a Weezer band tee, with no bra. Her small nipples pressed against the loose fabric. Her pale legs glowed in the moonlight.

"Marnie, has anyone ever told you how beautiful you are?"

She made a strange sound in the back of her throat. "You don't mean that."

Charles wanted to slap her, but instead he reached a hand up to touch her cheek, lightly caressing the soft skin with his thumb. He smiled as she grew warm and pink beneath his fingers.

"Why would I lie to you?"

She parted her lips, as if to say something, but then closed them again.

"Marnie, can I kiss you?"

Her large eyes widened a fraction more.

Charles leaned in, slowly. Marnie stayed perfectly still as he brushed his lips against hers. He kissed her softly at first, and when she didn't object, he cupped her doll-like face in his hands. He coaxed her lips open with his tongue, licked the tops of her teeth. "I want you," he said.

"What do you mean?" she asked.

Charles laughed softly this time, brushing her bottom lip with his thumb. He scanned the yard, his eyes falling on the old tree house that hadn't been touched in years. Standing, he took Marnie's hand and pulled her up with him. "I'll show you."

Marnie didn't protest as he pulled her across the shadowed lawn, into the black of night.

anxious preoccupied

given the choice
I would have chosen her
over all else
like those baby monkeys
in Harry Harlow's study of attachment
I would have starved to death
for her affection

To Me, She is Already Everything

Simone and I are leaning towards one another across a small, round table at the coffee house. Like a reflex, my hand reaches up to tuck a stray piece of hair behind her ear. I'm so mesmerized by her—the way her eyes sparkle like clear blue pools of water, the way her cheeks flush pale pink when my fingertips brush against her skin—I don't notice anyone else come into the coffee house, don't hear the footsteps approaching, until it's too late.

"Who the fuck is this?" The menacing voice behind me asks, loud enough that everyone in the small café turns to stare.

Simone straightens up immediately. Her face drains of color and her eyes widen with fear. "N-no one." He takes a step forward, his eyes on me, and I imagine I feel as prey must feel, as the predator stalks in for the kill. Simone jumps up quickly, positioning herself between us. Meanwhile, I remain immobilized in my chair. "He's no one, Vincent."

I want to believe that she's only trying to protect me, but her words cut into me like knives. He's *no one.* I realize in this moment, that to her, I *am* no one—just some kid she barely knows—while to me, she is already everything. My stomach twists into knots and I feel like I'm going to be sick.

"The fuck he's no one," Vincent sneers. His fists are clenched so tightly the knuckles are white.

"He's just a kid," Simone tries to reason, placing her hands on his chest.

Vincent grunts and uses one arm to move Simone out of the way. "If I *ever* catch you near my girlfriend again, I don't care how young you are, I will beat you until the features on your face are unrecognizable."

When I say nothing, too terrified to move, he grabs the collar of my shirt and pulls me up until I'm standing, my face inches from his. "Do you understand?"

I nod my head, unable to speak.

He gives me one last threatening glare and then turns toward Simone. "We're leaving," he says, and taking her wrist in his hand, he drags her towards the door. She looks back at me with a desperate look in her eyes, and mouths, *I'm sorry*, before she disappears.

to Winter

outside her window spiderweb branches crawl
across a darkening sky—the cold, wet, white
makes faces in the glass—the light bulbs
emit their white light—the radiator creaks, like bones
snapping, and the dry hot keeps pumping, but
it isn't getting any warmer, and she keeps flipping
the switch in her mind, to no effect, while Winter
whispers softly in her ear, *sleep now*
with his cold, wet lips

The Little Blue Demon

No one knew exactly what went on at *Corrections*, except for those who had been there. The girls who came back were so thin, weightless as paper. Their cheeks were gaunt, their eyes ghoulish. They kept their heads down, jumped like frightened cats if you caught them off guard, and would say nothing—no matter how adamantly you pressed them—of what had been done to them there.

Anne was sure that if she was sent there, she would be one of those girls who simply disappeared, one of those girls no one ever heard from again. There were rumors about what *The Association* did with the girls who were deemed unfit for re-assimilation into society. Some said they were sent to dimly lit brothels where no one really had to look at them, where men paid almost nothing to fuck them any way they pleased. Others said they just lined them up and picked them off one by one—sent a bullet clean through the center of their foreheads. Still others insisted they harvested their organs for the sick and wealthy, or used them as guinea pigs for new medical research.

Until a couple months ago, Anne would have laughed at the idea of being sent to *Corrections*. Anne wasn't beautiful—not like her best friend Sammy—but she was pretty enough, and she had always managed to stay skinny. That is, until she came home one afternoon on her lunch break and caught her boyfriend of three years fucking her next-door neighbor on the kitchen counter.

Since then, Anne had been on a downward spiral. She knew it was *weak* and *pathetic* to let herself go—or at least, that's what Sammy told her. "You need to make him sorry, show him what he's missing out on," she would say—but Anne couldn't help it. Every morning when her alarm went off, a little blue demon came to sit on her chest, preventing her from getting out of bed. There was nothing she could do but wait for him to leave.

Of course, she couldn't tell Sammy—couldn't tell anyone—about the little blue demon. They wouldn't understand. They would say she was making it up. But she wasn't. He was real, and *he* was responsible for Anne's sudden weight gain, for the itchy, red rash spreading across her skin.

She had tried pleading with him, begging him to go away. But instead of deterring him, her tears made him grow. He drank them up like holy water. His belly became as round as the Buddha's, until he was so heavy Anne could barely breathe. Sometimes she would wake up in the night gasping for air and crawl on her hands and knees to the bathroom, where she would rest her face on the cool tiles until the sun came up.

At work Anne felt like a Barbie doll with a painted smile, spinning endlessly in circles, repeating the same phrases over and over. She'd been a waitress since graduating from high school. It was supposed to have been temporary. She had planned on saving up money to go to Art school—like Sammy—but somehow time had slipped out from under her. Before she knew it, three years had gone by, then four, then five. The restaurant, as much as she loathed it, had become a part of her, and she didn't know who she would be if she left, or where she would go, or who, if anyone, would even have her.

"I don't know what I'm going to do," Anne moaned into Sammy's cream-colored sofa.

Sammy had been flitting about her apartment all afternoon, fussing over every little detail. For the last twenty minutes—Anne had been watching the clock—Sammy had been polishing her already-glowing mahogany coffee table.

"You can stop feeling sorry for yourself, for one," Sammy said.

Anne sighed. Sammy—who was so completely perfect, with her slim, supple body, flawless skin, and silky obsidian hair—couldn't understand what Anne was going through.

"I mean it, Anne. You've got to stop whining and get off your ass. You're not going to lose the weight lying on my sofa like some pathetic, wounded animal."

Anne's face went bright, tomato red.

When Sammy saw Anne's face, she put down the cloth she was using to polish the coffee table and came to sit next to her on the couch. "I'm sorry, that was a little harsh. I'm just so stressed out about my date tonight. I want everything to be perfect, but my apartment is a disaster, and I've been inexplicably bloated all afternoon."

"Don't be ridiculous, Sammy. You are beautiful and perfect, and your apartment is like something out of a *Designer Homes* magazine." Anne had always been jealous of Sammy's apartment— the cypress floors, elegant furniture, and exquisite paintings lining the walls, all gave it the air of an upscale art gallery—much like the one where Sammy worked as a curator.

Sammy kissed the top of Anne's head. "Thanks, doll."

Anne smiled her best painted smile for Sammy.

"Have you been taking those vitamins I gave you?" Sammy asked, twirling a piece of Anne's limp, beige hair between her fingers.

"Yeah," Anne lied. They had been sitting in her cupboard for weeks, untouched. The little blue demon wouldn't let her take them.

Sammy coughed.

"Why?" Anne asked in an attempt to stir the stale air.

Sammy shrugged. "No reason."

The room went quiet again. Anne's attention shifted to the sound of cars driving on the street below, the electric hum of the city, the place Anne had always called home. "So, is this the same guy you went on a date with last week, or a different one?"

Sammy laughed. "The same. His name is Chad."

"Chad. Right. Did you say he works for *The Association?*"

"Yes. He's the head of the *Department of Regulations*."

Anne's body stiffened. "Oh."

Sammy nodded. "That's why I'm so nervous."

Anne sat up on the sofa and hugged her knees to her chest. "I'm sure he's already madly in love with you."

"Don't be stupid, Anne," Sammy said, standing up abruptly. "Men like Chad can snap their fingers and have any woman they want."

"I'm sorry, I didn't—"

Sammy cut her off. "You should go. Chad will be here soon." Her eyes were glowing like embers. To Anne she looked like a beautiful and dangerous goddess of destruction. Chad didn't stand a chance.

"Oh," Anne said, clearing her throat. "You don't want to introduce us?"

The look Sammy gave Anne was saturated with pity. "Maybe when you're a little more . . . presentable," she said.

The words stung Anne like a slap.

Sammy turned away, her face hardening into cold lines.

Anne got up and walked out of the apartment without a word.

On the street Anne could feel everyone's eyes on her. The sexy blonde, walking her Pomeranian in black stilettos turned her nose up at Anne in distaste. The man in a lavender suit skirted around Anne as though her despair were contagious.

She walked quickly with her head down. Too late, she noticed a couple of patrolmen standing in the middle of the sidewalk just up ahead. She turned—without looking—to cross the street and walked right into a woman pushing a pram. The impact made her infant cry out in shrieks of terror.

The mother, with her perfectly made up face, and chocolate brown hair in tight curls, looked at Anne with murder in her eyes. "My baby!" she wailed.

Before Anne knew what was happening, she felt a hand around the top of her arm, yanking her away from the mother and baby.

"What's going on here?" one of the patrolmen asked, his voice deep and dry like cracked leather.

"This *woman*," the mother spat, "*ran* into me and my baby!"

"I'm sorry, I'm *so* sorry," Anne said, her whole body prickling with fear.

The patrolmen, menacing in their black armoured uniforms, looked her up and down.

"Is that true?" asked the patrolman, who was still gripping her tightly by the arm. His eyes were a cold, piercing blue. He was considerably younger than the other patrolman, perhaps not much older than Anne.

Anne's vision blurred. She felt dizzy. "It was an accident! I'm sorry, I'm really, really sorry."

"*Sorry*?! Do you think my *baby*, my *poor*, traumatized, *baby*, cares if you're *sorry*?" The woman was on the edge of hysterics.

"Alright, ma'am," the senior patrolman said.

Anne could see a flash of dismay cross his face.

The infant's relentless screeching was drawing curious stares from passersby. The spell of peace and tranquility cast so deftly by *The Association*, was being broken.

"Let's take a walk," the senior patrolman continued to the woman. "You can calm your baby down, and we'll get this sorted."

The woman stiffened, remembering her place. "Yes, sir. Of course."

The senior patrolman looked from Anne, to his comrade. "You got this?"

"I'll handle it, sir."

"Good," the senior patrolman said. "I'll see you back at high command."

"Yes, sir," said the young patrolman.

"Alright, ma'am," the senior patrolman said to the woman, "I'm going to escort you home now."

"Yes, sir."

Anne and the young patrolman watched as they walked briskly down the street and disappeared around a corner.

The patrolman turned his eyes on Anne.

The air around her chilled.

Ice—his eyes were the color of ice. His face was only inches from hers.

She couldn't meet his gaze.

Seconds passed, and still, he said nothing. Anne felt like she was going to be sick.

"Sir, I, I'm so—"

The patrolman smirked then. "You're a bit of a mess, aren't you?"

"Sir, I—"

"Shhhh," the patrolman said, putting a finger to her lips. "You've been crying." With his thumb, he wiped the tears from first one cheek, and then the other. His skin was cool and soft.

Every muscle in Anne's body tightened.

The patrolman cleared his throat. He took Anne's left wrist in his hand and rotated her arm so that her palm was facing up, exposing the barcode on her identification bracelet. He pulled a device from the holster on his belt and scanned it. The monitor on the device lit up.

"Ah," he said, as though suddenly everything was clear. "Anne Adler. 24. Residence: 701 Moss Drive Apt. #14. Graduated in the top ten from Hyde Preparatory School for Girls. No college degree. Current Occupation: Waitress at *Fuel.* Previous Infractions: None."

Anne's eyes burned. She wanted to cry, to collapse, to disappear. She was willing to do whatever it took to make this end, if only she knew how.

The patrolman lifted Anne's chin, so she was forced to meet his gaze. There was something dancing in those ice colored eyes— malice? Bemusement? Prurience? Anne couldn't be sure.

"What are we going to do with you, Miss Adler?"

A chill ran up Anne's spine.

"Assault. Disturbance of the peace. Unsightly public appearance. These are serious offenses."

"Sir, please, I—" Anne couldn't hold the tears back any longer—they spilled in hot streams down her cheeks. "I'll do anything."

The patrolman smiled.

Anne understood now—she was familiar with this dance.

The patrolman wiped the tears from her face once more. "Now there, sweetheart, don't cry. Let's get you home."

He wrapped his arm around her body, and Anne deflated into him, her body flooding with relief.

After he left, Anne lay in her bed, her chest a hollow cavern. The little blue demon came—as Anne knew he would. He stayed with her all night, while Anne stared into the darkness, consumed with one singular image.

It was not of the patrolman licking his lips as he plunged himself into her, but of Sammy—of the absent look on her face when she told Anne that she wasn't good enough for her.

désirer

it is Edith   singing
je ne regrette rien   and *la vie en rose*
after sex   in the midsummer heat
of your apartment   above the garage
in the valley—   playing Scrabble
and a bottle   of prosecco
wearing nothing   but your t-shirt.
It is bubbles   tingling
on my lips   and tongue
and the inside   of my cheeks,
the way you shake   your head when you look
at me, and close your   eyes, and breathe
in when I touch   your skin with the tips
of my fingers.   It is a cold
walk home   in late September.
It is all the words   I want to say,
but can't.   It is the chickadee
on the other side   of the window,
flitting   from branch
to branch in the pale   morning sun

Wait for Me

Kate really wasn't the snooping type. She resented David for forcing her hand. If he were only honest with her, it wouldn't be necessary. As it was, she knew he was keeping something—or rather, some *one*—from her, and she was going to find out what or *who* it was.

She didn't believe his story about staying late after school to tutor struggling students. Perhaps if it was only one or two days a week, she wouldn't have given it a second thought, but he'd been staying late—sometimes two or three hours after school—every *day* for months now. No one was that selfless, least of all her husband.

She had spent the better part of her morning ruffling through his office—looking for anything the least bit suspicious. She had even managed to get into his email account, but there was nothing there. Nonetheless, she was still convinced that he was sleeping with another woman—a fellow teacher, or perhaps one of the office secretaries. A teacher was more likely, though. David preferred intellectual women, in a way that most men didn't. He liked to be challenged—to have his *mental faculties aroused,* as he would say.

Kate had always harbored the suspicion that David held it against her for dropping out of college early. He had proposed in her junior year, and after that, she just hadn't seen the point in finishing. She wanted to be a stay-at-home mom, and since the whole idea of college was to be able to get a job afterwards— which she had no intention of doing—the whole charade seemed like a perfect waste of time. The only reason she had gone to college in the first place was to meet an attractive, intelligent man, whom her parents would approve of, and she had done just that.

David had begun to realize the kind of woman Kate was much too late. The sickeningly extravagant wedding her father was paying for had only been weeks away when the enormity of his error in judgement dawned on him. Something about the way Kate's father clapped him on the shoulder and said, "All men get cold feet before they get married, son. Don't you worry. It will all be over soon," had made him think he would not be permitted to simply walk away.

Kate had wanted to start a family almost immediately after they were married, but David had managed to convince her to hold off a while, insisting that he wanted to wait until they were more settled. "I'm not ready to share you quite yet," he had told her, which couldn't have been further from the truth. To his immense relief, when they had eventually started trying, nothing had happened, and the noose around his neck gradually began to loosen.

Fortunately, being married to Kate wasn't the *worst* thing in the world. She kept herself busy with endless lunch dates, yoga classes, and hair appointments—requiring very little of him. Only asking the bare minimum—*Come pose for this photo, Darling. My parents want to get lunch next week, Darling. Can you zip up my dress, Darling?*

It was inside the pocket of one of his suit coats, hanging unassumingly in the closet, that Kate found what she was looking for—a folded up piece of notebook paper. Written in small sloping letters were two lines.

> *My head is full of you.*
> *Wait for me.*
>
> *-M*

M, m, m, m, m . . . Kate turned the letter over and over in her mind. Who was *M*? She went to David's desk, where there was a neat pile of essays waiting to be graded. It was right there, on the top of the pile, in the upper left-hand corner—*Marnie Miller.*

residue

her mind buzzes—*bzz bzz bzz*—like a bumble bee can't sleep
she gives me a silver, feather-carved ring and tells me to love
myself at the bar we drown
our self-hatred in beer and curly fries coat our insides with a thick
greasy residue she tells me her ex-husband abused her
how she thinks about killing herself because my cousin won't
return her calls—2 years, for nothing she snaps me pictures of her
puffy face he tells me he's tired of chasing her over bagels
with his mother at Java Joe's
I sip my creamy cold brew, and listen
scrape the excess cream cheese off my pumpernickel bagel

First Kiss

The night air is cool, and it bites my face as I ride along the darkened streets. My skin prickles with anticipation. I grip the handlebars tightly, so my hands won't shake.

My stomach does somersaults as I realize this will probably be my last chance to impress her. Tonight, is a test. I will either pass or fail.

I lock my bike to a wooden post at the edge of the beach, which is pale and expansive in the moonlight.

Simone is sitting in the sand, her body a smudge against the otherwise perfect smoothness. I walk towards her slowly, afraid that if I move too quickly, she will vanish.

She looks up, smiles as I approach her. "Hey, Leo."

"Hey, Simone," I say as I sit down next to her.

The moonlight casts eerie shadows on her face.

She watches me watching her. "What are you thinking about?"

I laugh, embarrassed. "I can't tell you."

She nudges my shoulder with her shoulder. "Now you have to."

"Oh?"

"Yes! You could have said, 'Nothing,' like everyone always does, but you didn't."

"Why would I say 'Nothing' when that's such an obvious lie?"

"Lying doesn't seem to bother most people."

"Well . . ." I pause, searching for the right words. "Lying to my mother or teachers is one thing, but I'd be stupid to lie to you."

"What makes you say that?"

"When you look at me . . ."

"Yes?"

"I feel like you're seeing right through me."

She tilts her head back and laughs.

"No, really. I get the feeling there isn't much that gets by you. I see the way you look at the world, like you understand it, like you see so much more than everyone else sees . . ."

She says nothing, only stares back at me with wide eyes.

I reach up to caress her cheek with my thumb. She closes her eyes. I lean in until our faces are only inches apart.

"Would you be mad if I kissed you?"

Instead of answering, she closes the gap between our faces, and presses her lips to mine. I cup her face in my hands. She places a palm flat against my chest with one hand and grabs a handful of hair at the back of my head with the other.

She runs her tongue along my bottom lip and I groan.

I move a hand to her back and gently push her down, so she is lying in the sand. I reposition my body over hers, kiss her neck, her chest . . . I lift her shirt, and a strangled noise escapes my throat. Her stomach and rib cage are a mosaic of bruises in varying shades and stages. Dots and smudges of blue and purple, mixed with ones of yellow and brown, like a child's finger painting.

"Don't," she whispers.

I look up to meet her wary gaze. My mouth hangs open as I stutter.

"Please, don't say anything, Leo. Can you do that for me?"

I nod my head once.

She moves her hand to pull her shirt back down, but I place my hand over hers.

"Leo," she protests.

I ignore her. Bringing my face to her abdomen, I gently, lovingly, kiss a small purple bruise. Then, the yellow one next to it, and the brown one next to that one. I work my way from one to the next, until I have kissed each one.

When I look back up at Simone, she is staring up at the stars, silent tears spilling from her eyes.

I lay my body next to hers and pull her onto my chest.

She buries her face in my shirt and cries quietly, while I rub her back and kiss the top of her head.

I think the question, "Why don't you leave him?" over and over in my mind, but I can't bring myself to ask it.

dream poem

last night I dreamt there were dozens
of dead bodies in my room. I cut them into
pieces. I thought I could bury them but
there were too many, so I dropped their limbs
one by one into a barrel of acid and watched
their flesh fizzle and dissolve

A Questionnaire

1. When women talk about their menstrual cycles in my presence I feel:

    a. deeply offended; women's bodily functions are disgusting

    b. confused; what's a menstrual cycle?

    c. so uncomfortable I have to stick my fingers in my ears and yell *la la la!* to drown them out

    d. honored and privileged that the women in my life choose to discuss the beautiful, natural cycles of their bodies with me

2. My opinion on period sex:

    a. fuck no; go into the woods with a bucket, and don't come out until you're no longer bleeding out of your vagina like a diseased animal

    b. undecided

    c. only in the shower

    d. I'm a grown ass man who isn't bothered by getting a little blood on my dick

3. Where I stand on going down on women:

    a. fuck no; the mere thought of going down on a woman makes me want to puke

b. do women really like that?

c. only after she's showered

d. I'd eat her pussy all day, every day if she let me

Results:

mostly a) in this case, a stands for Grade A asshole. Do humanity a favor and slither back into the mud you crawled out of.

mostly b) you are either much too young to be reading this, or you are the dumbest human male on the planet.

mostly c) you are arguably worse than the Grade A asshole. You are a little boy inhabiting a grown man's body. Women date you because they feel sorry for you. They think they can educate you, that you will inevitably have to grow up one day, but 10 years and three kids later, you'll still be getting drunk every Sunday, screaming at football from the living room couch, and she'll be taking yoga classes and drinking wine with her girlfriends on the weekends, lamenting about how unhappy she is, how invisible she feels, wondering how her life turned out so terribly, terribly wrong.

mostly d) you are every woman's dream, you are the hope that keeps strong, intelligent, straight women, from giving up on men entirely, but the terrible, awful truth is—you don't exist, and if you do, you're married, or you're not ready to get serious, or you are otherwise unavailable.

Familiar Face

Sitting at the bar with your aunt on a Friday night reminds you how desperate you are for friends your own age. So you drink your tequila and ginger soda cocktail a little bit faster than you should. You have to remind yourself to keep smiling, so she doesn't think you're having a miserable time.

When your aunt's ex-boyfriend walks into the bar with a couple of friends, you and your aunt go over to say hello. By now you're on your second drink and the world is blurry, yet focused. You blame feeling more drunk than you reasonably should on your new diet of bananas and vegetables. The bar is getting louder and warmer, but you see nothing beyond the four people sitting at the table in front of you.

You get so animated telling a story to one of the friends of your aunt's ex—the one sitting closest to you, who is pudgy and has a beard, who you think is probably around thirty-five, and who definitely wants to fuck you—that you fall backwards out of your chair, hitting your head on the table behind you, but you're so drunk that you barely feel it, and you get right back up again and laugh at yourself for being so basic.

You continue to tell the story, the one you started before you fell, about the self-study astrologist back in Boulder who offered to trade you an astrology reading for a massage. You emphasize how much this offended you, because as a licensed massage therapist, you have an actual skill.

When your aunt and her ex-boyfriend and his friends are all ready to leave, you insist on staying, even though you know you shouldn't. After they've gone, you go up to the bar and order another tequila with ginger soda. You start up a conversation with the guy to your right who is also ordering a drink, or maybe he's just closing his tab. He tells you his name, but you forget it almost

70

immediately. He has black hair down past his ears like Adam Driver. You exchange stories about the time you both spent in Colorado and he tells you about his job making snowboards up at the loaf.

He says he has to work in the morning, but offers to walk you back to your apartment, which you've already told him is just around the corner and up the street. You agree to let him, even though you aren't ready to go home yet. It's cold outside, but the alcohol has made you too numb to feel it. It would be dark, but the street lamps shine bright downtown. In a moment, you're standing in front of the door to your building with this guy whose name you can't remember, and you're not sure how you got there so quickly.

You invite him to come upstairs, but he says he really has to go. You try to convince him, beg him, to come up just for a moment—which you'll hate yourself for when you're sober—because you can't bear to face your empty apartment alone. When he turns you down for the second time, or maybe it's the third, you try to pretend like the rejection doesn't sting, but you know he knows it does, because even when you're sober, you're not very good at pretending.

Isolated in your apartment, with the baby blue kitchen and lavender bedroom—colors you picked out yourself—your head spins so bad that the thought of lying down makes you nauseated. So you check your face in the mirror—the long green one you got from your best friend when she was moving out of her dorm room and couldn't fit it in her car—before you head back out into the night.

It feels colder now as you half-walk, half-run down the hill back into town, anxious not to be alone with yourself. In your haste, you slip on a patch of ice and land hard on your right knee, but this you don't really feel either. The rest of the night starts to break down into time elapsed fragments, like the footage from a camera that only takes pictures every ten seconds. You find yourself in the only bar in town still open this late, but you don't remember walking down the carpeted flight of stairs to get to this room that smells like beer and sweat, crowded with other inebriated bodies.

Drunk, lonely you searches the room for a familiar face, and finds one in the distant corner, to the left of the bar. Your sister's ex-boyfriend's younger brother who was a year ahead of you in high school. The guy you sat next to in a class about Shakespeare, who never seemed to like you very much, but you walk right over to him anyway.

You lean up against an arcade game machine and talk about things you won't remember in the morning. When the lights come on and everyone starts to leave, he walks you home and you don't even have to ask him to come in with you.

november

the snow floats down from
the white Boulder sky
in thick, lazy clumps
as he tells me we can't see
each other anymore,
"I don't want you," he says,
"to get feelings for me
that I can't reciprocate."

Cold Tea

We agreed to meet at five-thirty on a Tuesday. He let me pick the location—a small café I frequented often. I wanted it to be somewhere familiar, somewhere I felt comfortable.

I arrived early, giving myself time to check my face in the restroom mirror. I wanted him to see me and think that I must be doing well, but my tired reflection told a different story. I had aged since I saw him last. Lines had formed on my face—etched there by sorrow and worry.

I was only twenty-one, but I felt infinitely older. The girl he knew was someone I had once been in a different life. She believed that the world was abundant with love, that love would be waiting for her around every corner.

After nearly three years of silence, he had sent me a casual message, *Hey, how are you?*

When I asked if he would like to meet up, he agreed. I wasn't expecting him to, considering that during our last conversation I told him exactly how little I thought of his new girlfriend, to which his reply had been, "Anyone is better than you."

Most people, I think, would have been deeply hurt by such a remark, but I had felt strangely triumphant. Someone has to love you an awful lot to feel that degree of animosity. It's not the type of thing you say to just anyone—it's the type of thing you say to someone whom you love beyond reason, someone who's hurt you so badly, you would say or do anything to make them feel half as much pain as you do.

I sat at a small table by the window, sipping tea. I was looking down into the cup, carefully examining the deep green tea leaves, when I heard a familiar, "Hey."

I looked up to see him staring down at me. He was as handsome as ever, although skinnier than the last time I had seen him. He had lost the boyish roundness from his face—the boyish roundness I had once loved. Now in its place were the hollowed cheekbones and hard jawline of a man.

"Hey," I breathed, and without any conscious thought I stood and hugged him, as though it were the most natural thing in the world.

For a second, he didn't move. I held my breath—worried I had overstepped—but then he wrapped his arms around me. I breathed all of him in, in one hungry inhalation, and I felt like I was finally home, after being away for a very, very long time.

He pulled away after a moment, and as my eyes met his, I saw that his expression had changed. There was something bubbling up under the pretense of being happy to see me.

He sat down across from me.

"You look beautiful," he said.

A golf ball-sized lump formed in the base of my throat.

He took one of my hands in both of his, and said, "I've missed you."

I tried to form words, but my lips remained pressed firmly together while my tongue moved like a dumb, blind worm in the dark cavity of my mouth.

His features were suddenly cruel. He squeezed my hand so tightly it hurt, but I said nothing, because the pain felt good and right.

"Why did you want to see me?" he asked.

I shook my head. I was far too much of a coward to say the words I wanted to say to him.

He sighed, more disappointed than angry, and checked his watch. "I should get home. Heather will be expecting me."

"I'm sorry," I whispered.

He hesitated for a moment.

I held my breath, waiting.

He opened his mouth, and then closed it, and I saw the resolution solidify in his eyes, like a vault door closing and latching into place. He shook his head and walked away.

As I watched him go, every nerve and muscle fiber in my body screamed at me to run after him, to tell him how I felt.

When he disappeared from view, my eyes dropped to the cup of cold tea cradled in my hands.

I envisioned him coming home to Heather, wrapping her up in his arms and kissing her with purpose—trying to work the memory of me from his mind. He would breathe all of her in, trying to forget the way I smelled.

As he made love to her, he would keep his eyes closed. She would sense that something was off, but say nothing—thinking it was only a stressful day at work on his mind.

Paper cut-out

"I just want paper cut-outs to love me,"
he says, as I moan into the phone and
he jerks off in a Subway restroom, and
I tell him about the sex I had the day
before with the engineer who held my
hands above my head when I told him
to stop and *Wedding Crashers* played
intermittently between commercials.

Please, Call Me Alberta

Alberta never intended to cheat on her husband, and certainly not with her son's childhood best friend. The boys were home from college for the holidays. Charles seemed so mature and dignified at the New Year's Eve party his parents threw every year. He was handsome and charming and wouldn't stop peppering her with compliments.

"Mrs. Jefferson, you look ravishing tonight," Charles said. "Can I get you another drink?"

"Please, call me Alberta."

"Can I get you another drink, Alberta?"

She was already on her third, but no matter. What were the holidays for, if not getting sloshed *sans* judgement or consequences? Besides, her husband had been making a show of flirting with the recently divorced Mrs. Norton.

The poor woman, Alberta thought. It had turned out that not only had Mr. Norton been sleeping with one of his students, but he had also managed to get her pregnant. What really confounded Alberta, the part she found the most contemptible about the whole situation—when Mrs. Norton had confronted him—he hadn't even tried to deny it. It was as though he had been waiting for her to find out, and *then*, just like that, the bastard had gone and run away with his sixteen-year-old, pregnant student.

During those interminable hours of the night when sleep so cruelly eluded Alberta, she found herself thinking of them. Where had they gone? What kind of life were they living? Had they changed their names? Created new identities for themselves? She mused how Mr. Norton had been lucky—or perhaps he had merely been clever—that he had not chosen to sleep with a student from a wealthy family, who surely would have hired a private detective to find and return their precious daughter.

Ruminating over the lives of others allowed Alberta a much-needed reprieve from sorting through the banal details of her own life. Mrs. Norton was laughing garishly at something her husband had said—something she surely would have found trite or insipid. Rather than feel anger or annoyance, she felt pity for them. They both seemed to be so desperate, grasping for something that was always just out of reach.

Harold, her husband, had been trying so ardently to rekindle the spark between them. He had thought things might get better once their son, James, left for college. To his dismay, they hadn't. The truth was, Alberta no longer found herself attracted to her husband. At fifty, Harold was really beginning to lose his sexual appeal. His hair had begun to thin and gray, his muscles were slowly atrophying, and his gut distending.

Alberta, on the other hand, looked absolutely stunning for a woman of forty-seven. Unlike her husband, she worked hard to remain young and beautiful for as long as she possibly could. She attended Pilates and spin classes several times per week, and had even started attending a weekly pole fitness class with one of her more adventurous friends.

Alberta was frustrated with her husband for not seeming to care in the slightest about his physical appearance. She supposed that's how it tended to go for men. Their value wasn't tied to their looks or youthfulness as a woman's was.

As the Dean of a university, Harold was certainly a successful man. In fact, he had all the things most men only dreamt of—a beautiful wife, who had been an excellent mother and homemaker, a rewarding and lucrative career, and a brilliant son who was studying to be a doctor at Yale. The only missing piece to the impressive mosaic of Harold's life, was a wife who wanted to have sex with him.

Alberta was surprised at how little resistance she felt within herself as Charles had pulled her up the stairs of his parents' house, towards his bedroom. She felt that she should have been ashamed or disgusted with herself as she tore the clothes off a boy who was the same age as her son. Instead, the taboo and wrongness of it only made it that much more thrilling. His body was long and lean, sculpted from years of religious athleticism. His skin was smooth beneath her hands, and he was hard before she even touched him. The way he fucked her, with a hungry insistence, made her feel more alive than she had felt in years.

chimera

I saw him, in the grocery store
the other day—bathed in the brilliant
clarity of fluorescent light
our eyes met, and I was at once
the little girl who loved him, and the
grown woman who'd spent years
scrubbing him away

Morgan Jackel

Out of necessity I've made friends with a boy named Ellis. He's in my French and history classes, and we have the same lunch period, so it worked out nicely. He's intelligent and friendly, and only moderately annoying.

Today, we're sitting at our usual lunch table in the corner.

"So, what's going on with you and Morgan Jackel?" Ellis asks out of the blue.

"Huh?" I reply, my mouth full of the turkey sandwich my mother had packed in my lunchbox.

"Don't play dumb with me. She hasn't stopped staring at you since we sat down."

I finish chewing and swallow. "Yeah, I noticed," I say, shrugging my shoulders.

Ellis is getting impatient with me. "Okay, so what's going on?"

"Nothing. Honest. She gave me her number and invited me to a party last week. I think she might be into me or something."

"And you're not into her?" Ellis is staring at me now like I've just said the most ridiculous thing he's ever heard.

I shrug. "I don't know. Not really, I guess."

"Are you gay?"

I choke. A mixture of saliva and little droplets from the water I was drinking land on the table. "What? No."

"Are you sure? 'Cause Morgan is a fucking smoke show, *and* she's a cheerleader. Most guys at this school would give their left nut to get with her."

"She's alright. Seems kind of basic, though."

Ellis rolls his eyes at me. Then his expression changes, like something has just clicked. "You're into someone else, aren't you?"

I take another bite of my sandwich and shrug.

"Who is she? Does she go to school here? Or is she back in Portland?"

I sigh. Ellis doesn't seem likely to quit with the interrogation anytime soon, so I decide it will be better for everyone involved if I just give in now. "Her name is Simone. She works at the coffee shop in town."

"Ellis, I really don't think this is a good idea. I don't even know if she's working today," I say, as Ellis and I lock our bikes up, down the street from the coffee house.

"Relax. We're just getting coffee," Ellis says as he starts walking up the street.

I exhale, exasperated, but follow him anyway. "She's going to think I'm stalking her."

Ellis laughs. "That's a possibility. But you know, some girls are really into that."

He looks back at me, smiling as he opens the coffee house door.

I glare at him in return.

"Wow, this place is nice. I can't believe I've never been in here before."

I make a kind of "mmm yeah" noise in response as I scan the coffee house for Simone. When I don't see her behind the counter, I'm simultaneously disappointed and relieved.

Ellis makes his way to the counter and I trail behind him.

"Leee-o!" Someone calls in a high-pitched voice from behind me.

"Fuck," I whisper under my breath.

Ellis turns around. "Oh, hey Morgan!"

I reluctantly turn around to face her, wishing instead I could make myself invisible.

"Hey, Leo," she says, flashing her milk-white teeth. She's wearing shimmering, Barbie-doll-pink lip gloss, and her blonde hair is in pigtails. "Who's your friend?"

"I'm Ellis," he says, saving me the trouble, and holds out his hand for her to shake.

She places her long, pink finger-nailed hand in his. "Very nice to meet you, Ellis." Her voice is far too sweet to be genuine. In fact, her whole person oozes insincerity.

"Likewise. I mean, I know of you, of course, but it's nice to be formally meeting you," he says.

She smiles brightly before turning back to me. "So, what brings you here, Leo?"

"Coffee," I say. "You?"

"Just picking up some skinny iced lattes for me and the girls before practice," she says, twirling the hem of her uniform. It's purple and white—Nesika High School colors.

"Nice."

"You and your friend can come watch, if you want."

Before I am able to say no, Ellis says, "We'd love to."

I open my mouth in opposition, but Morgan responds before I am able to make any sounds come out.

"Great! We're working on a new routine for the game Friday night, and could really use some feedback."

"For sure, we'd be more than happy to help," Ellis says.

I want to slap the stupid grin off his face.

"I've got an order for Morgan. Three skinny iced lattes." The skin on the back of my neck prickles at the sound of her voice. She must have been out back when we walked in.

Morgan touches my arm and says, "That's me. See you soon, Leo."

I nod without looking at her and turn around. Simone is wearing her hair in a high ponytail today. She looks tired, and a little sad.

Morgan steps around me and Ellis to pick up her lattes, effectively blocking my view of Simone. Her pigtails bounce up and down obnoxiously as she moves.

Ellis nudges me in the ribs, and then says under his breath, "Dude, is that her? Is that Simone?"

"Yeah," I say, smiling at the look of comprehension forming on his face.

"She's beautiful," he exhales.

"Yeah, she is."

"Bye boys," Morgan says, as she walks by us with her tray of iced lattes.

I don't even glance in her direction.

Simone has noticed me now. Smiling, she says, "Can't get enough, can you?"

I shake my head as I approach the counter, Ellis at my heels. "Nope."

Ellis clears his throat next to me.

Taking the hint, I say, "This is my friend, Ellis."

"Hey, Ellis, I'm Simone. Can I get you gentlemen some coffee?"

"Yes, please," I reply, leaning on the counter. "Did you just get in?"

"Nah, I've been in since ten. I just got back from my lunch break."

"Oh. Cool, cool."

"Yeah, Vincent picked me up and we went for a ride."

My face falls at the mention of his name.

"Your girlfriend's cute," she says, catching me off guard.

"What? What girlfriend?"

"The cheerleader, silly. What was her name . . ."

"That's Morgan," Ellis pipes in. "She's not his girlfriend. Definitely has a crush on him, though."

"Clearly," Simone says laughing.

Ellis laughs too.

"I would *never* date a cheerleader," I say.

Simone looks at me sweetly. "I'm just teasing, Leo."

"Sure, sure," I say. "I just wouldn't want there to be any confusion." I look down at my feet, immediately embarrassed.

"So, what are you doing later?" Ellis asks Simone, coming to my rescue.

"I don't know," she says casually. "I get off at five . . . There's this movie playing I really want to see, but it's a romantic comedy, and Vincent would rather die than go with me."

"Leo will go with you," Ellis says.

I'm expecting Simone to say something along the lines of, *I wish I could, but Vincent would kill me.* Instead she says, "Really, Leo? You would?"

"Of course I would," I say. "But are you sure we should be seen out in public together?"

Simone shrugs, "Danger is the spice of life."

"I think you mean *variety* is the spice of life."

"Sure, that too," she says. "Meet me at the theater at seven?"

"I'll be there," I say.

She smiles. "You can come too, Ellis, if you'd like."

"He's busy," I say.

"Yeah. Big test tomorrow. Gotta study," he says.

"Okay," she says. "Let me get you gentlemen your coffee."

Outside, Ellis starts in. "I know you don't want to, but dude, can we pleeeease go watch the cheerleaders practice?"

I groan from deep in my throat.

"Come on, please, for me? I just got you a date with Simone."

I look at him and his sad pleading face for a long moment before I finally say, "Fine."

Dark blue clouds are forming in the sky like fresh bruises when we get to the football field, where Morgan and her minions are performing what I assume to be some sort of warm-up routine, in their sparkling mini-skirts.

Ellis walks up to the chain link fence bordering the field.

I hang back with our bikes and continue to study the cloud formations. "We shouldn't stay long," I say, more to myself than to Ellis.

He looks back at me. "Huh?"

"It looks like it's going to rain soon."

Ellis shrugs.

I sigh, and he turns his head back to the field.

A drop of rain hits my cheek.

Ellis looks back at me and I know he must have felt one too, because he is glaring at me as if I have summoned the rain.

I smile, and the sky opens. I hold my arms wide, letting the sheet of rain wash over me.

A chorus of high-pitched shrieks comes from the direction of the field, but it sounds far away.

"You look like a lunatic, smiling like that," Ellis says.

The shrieks and giggles descend upon us, shattering my moment of euphoria.

"I can't believe this," Morgan moans. "The weather forecast promised it wasn't going to rain until tonight." She is flanked on either side by two of her minions, the three of them looking like they're posing for *Teen Vogue*. Their nipples poke through the wet fabric of their white and purple uniform tops.

I close my eyes again, wishing I had the balls to be more like Tommy DeVito in *Jersey Boys*. How would Morgan react if I said, "I'll tell you what. I'm gonna shut my eyes and I'm gonna count to three. When I open them, you're gonna disappear." Would she actually walk away, all hurt and confused? Or would she slap me first? I always wondered if that kind of thing worked in real life.

Unfortunately, I am going to have to keep wondering, because Morgan asks, "So what did you think of the routine?" and my window of opportunity to find out closes with the shrill sound of her voice.

"You guys were *so* good," Ellis chimes in.

Morgan looks at me with her muddy-brown eyes, lids hooded in an effort to be seductive. "What did *you* think, Leo?"

I am tempted, for a brief moment, to give my honest opinion, but I instead go for the only acceptable answer I am capable of giving. "Yeah, same. Good."

If she is displeased with my answer, she doesn't let it show. "What are you boys doing tonight? I'm having a few friends over to my place."

The ridiculousness of it all is really starting to sink in. The five of us standing there in the downpour, Morgan trying desperately to carry on a conversation while her minions break formation and begin to shiver behind her, in their wet, skimpy uniforms.

"I have a prior engagement, actually, but Ellis is free."

Morgan's face falls visibly this time, but only for a second, before she puts a perfectly manicured hand on Ellis' shoulder and says, "Party starts at ten. See if you can convince him for me."

Ellis' pale cheeks pinken. "Yeah, uh, I'll see what I can do."

She smiles like the sly little minx she is, and trots off, minions at her tail.

"No," I say, as soon as they're out of earshot. "There's not a chance in hell." I lift my bicycle off the ground and mount it.

"I'll beg. If that's what you want, I'll do it." Ellis puts his hands together in front of him, like a child petitioning Mommy and Daddy for a puppy.

He looks pathetic with his soaked hair and rain splattered glasses. I can't help feeling sorry for him.

"Pleeee—"

"Okay! But *only* if Simone doesn't want to hang after the movie."

Ellis wraps his arms around me. "I fucking love you, man."

"You're such a Jerry," I grumble.

"A who?"

"Jerry, from *Rick and Morty.*"

"Oh. Ouch," he says, removing his arms from around my waist.

"Can I go now?"

"Sure. Go get spiffy for your date with Simone. I'll see you later."

"Maybe," I say, as I push off the ground and pedal away through the rain.

I stand in the parking lot of the movie theater for 45 minutes waiting for Simone to show up, before I finally decide she isn't coming. I get back on my bike and pedal furiously through the dark, quiet streets of downtown. She couldn't even be bothered to send a text? Do I really mean that little to her? Am I that inconsequential? That easily ignored and forgotten?

As my house comes into view, I pedal harder. I can't face my mother, can't bear the pity in her eyes telling me that Simone doesn't deserve me anyway.

The same question plays in my mind on a loop, as I bike up hill, after hill, welcoming the pain in my legs and lungs as I push myself harder and faster. How could she leave me standing out there like a fucking idiot?

I finally stop when I get to the lake. It's a windy night, and the black waves beat against the small square of sand beach with a ferocity that feels undeserved.

I throw my bike into the sand and bend over on my trembling legs to dry heave. Once I have caught my breath, I pull my phone out of my jacket pocket. It is nearly eight-thirty and still nothing from Simone.

I send Ellis a text. I'm coming over. Get booze.

The ride back into town is nearly all downhill. I take the corners fast, pedalling hard on the down slopes to catch as much speed as possible. The wind slaps my face as though it were punishing me for wanting too much, for wanting someone I can't have. The pain is cathartic. I want more. I want it to hurt so badly that my mind won't have the space or the energy to keep wondering—*why?*

Ellis opens the door before I knock. He has a glass of red wine in his hand, waiting for me.

I take the glass from him and drink it in the doorway in one long gulp.

If Ellis is concerned, he doesn't let it show. "Come inside, man. Take your shoes off. There's more where that came from."

Three more glasses of wine, a joint, and a couple hours later, and Ellis and I are walking through the dark streets of Nesika under the orange globes of lamp light to Morgan's house.

The air is cold and damp, and smells of rich, fresh earth, the way it always does after it rains.

Ellis and I walk in silence, until we're nearly to Morgan's, and he says, "So she didn't show up tonight, huh?"

"Nope."

"I'm sorry, man. Did she have a good excuse at least?"

"Nope. Didn't even bother to let me know she wasn't coming. I waited for her for almost an hour."

"Shit."

"Yup."

"Leo—"

"It's fine. Honestly. I just want to get fucked up tonight and forget it happened."

Morgan's house is large with big windows and a wrap-around porch supported by stone pillars. The air is electric, vibrating with music and teenage angst.

I go to knock on the door, but it's flung open from the inside before my knuckles make contact with the wood.

Morgan leans on the open door for support, already tipsy in her high-waisted skinny jeans and bright pink crop top. Her body is covered in a thin sheen of perspiration.

"Finally!" she squeals, leaning in to give me a sloppy, wet kiss on the cheek. "I was beginning to wonder if you were ever going to make it!" She smells like cheap beer and expensive perfume.

Ellis and I walk through the door and Morgan closes it behind us, teetering on her black pumps. "What can I get you boys to drink?"

I want to say, *Whatever is going to get us drunk quickest,* but instead I say, "Whatever you're drinking."

"Coming right up!" she says, motioning for us to follow behind her.

I look over at Ellis, but he's staring at Morgan's ass.

"Damn," he breathes.

I roll my eyes.

Ten minutes later, Morgan and I are sitting on a loveseat in the corner of her living room sipping keg beer from solo cups. She had introduced Ellis to a couple of her minions playing beer pong in the living room. I caught her wink at the redhead wearing too much eyeliner, who had immediately taken the hint and asked Ellis to join them.

"So, what do you think?" Morgan asks, batting her unnaturally long eyelashes.

"Of what?" I ask, already starting to wonder how soon is too soon to leave.

"The party, silly," she says, placing a hand on my thigh.

I look down at her pale, smooth fingers, glowing in the soft yellow mood-lighting. "It's not really my scene, to be honest," I say, downing the rest of my beer. "But I think another drink might help."

She squeezes my thigh and takes my cup. "Of course! I'll be right back. Don't go anywhere."

In the impressively short amount of time she is gone, I marvel at how girls like Morgan come to thrive on being treated like shit. The rich parents, maybe? Showering her with gifts and money, in lieu of their love and attention? Somehow making her desperate to impress someone like me—someone who reminds her of her parents, because I give equally little of a shit about her as they do?

Morgan comes back with two fresh solo cups, filled to the brim with something that isn't beer. She sloshes a bit of the clear, icy liquid on her jeans as she sits down.

"Whoops!" she giggles. "I thought you might like something a little stronger."

"Sure," I say, taking my cup.

"Don't you want to know what it is?"

I look at her, really look at her, for the first time. Something about the expression on her face, the pleading, pathetic look in her eyes, makes me want to shake her, tell her to wake up. I want to say to her, *None of this matters! Don't you see? Your fake friends, and your fake smile, and your fake fucking eyelashes—none of it matters! None of it is going to make you happy. None of it is going to make me like you, or make your parents like you. Nothing you do is going to change a goddamn thing.* But I just say, "Nope," and bring the cup to my lips, and tip it back until it is empty. Then I lean in close, so she can feel my hot breath on her neck, and say, "Isn't this the part where you invite me upstairs?"

Morgan locks her bedroom door behind us and tells me to sit on the bed. Everything in her room, from the bed to the walls, is in various shades of pink.

She kicks off her pumps and starts to strip slowly, until she is completely naked except for a gold, heart-shaped locket hanging in the hollow dip between her breasts. Her nipples are pale, pale pink, and her pussy is completely hairless.

"Your turn," she says.

I bend down to undo my shoelaces, but the motion makes me suddenly nauseated, and I puke all over her fluffy pink throw rug.

It is just after noon before I finally gather the strength—and the courage to face my mother—to bike home from Ellis' house. The sun is shining brilliantly in the cerulean blue September sky. The fresh air and the adrenaline from racing along the hilly roads back to my house remind me what it feels like to be alive.

I realize that I've been dream walking through the past couple of months. Since the day I walked into the coffee shop and met Simone, I've been in a daze. I haven't been seeing things clearly, and by things, what I mean is the one very real and unalterable fact that Simone doesn't give a shit about me. She looks at me the way I look at Morgan—like some sad, pathetic puppy dog she lets follow her around and feeds scraps to now and then out of pity.

How could I have been so stupid? How could I have allowed myself to believe there was a possibility she might actually like me? I'm a fucking idiot, that's how.

Things my mother told me in the winter of 2014

January 18th   You can't come   into the kitchen like that. We're being watched.   There's a camera in the stove.   What's fucking wrong   with you?   Who raised you?   You're disgusting. Stop bugging me.   Why are you still bugging me?   **January 21st** Why do you keep   staring at me?   You're making me suspicious like there are voices   in your head telling you   to stare at me. You know your father and Grammy were cremated.   I can feel them here   controlling me.   I don't like it it needs to stop!   **January 24th**   I work for the government. (pause)   I work for the FBI   and we're trying to bring down dogs like you.   **January 25th**   Let's go back   to pretending we were never   here and I never   knew you.   If I can make you hate me   I will be saved.   You know nothing   of salvation and you know nothing   of righteousness   or Jesus Christ or the blood of the lamb   and I do!   Because I read the Bible and I went to church   and Christian school!   All the Jews are going to hell!   If you keep eating   so many eggs you're going to get pregnant.   I will never hate you,   but I never want   to see you again.   You made me a bad mother. **January 26th**   I gave them colors.   I bet that's how it all started,   because I gave them colors.   **January 31st**

I hate you.   I've never hated anyone   as much as I hate you. You're just jealous   because I'm a better artist   than you. You've always been jealous   of me, and of Becky and Erick cause you could never be like us.   You're a fat pig.

Note: I copied down these words verbatim—at the suggestion of my high school creative writing teacher—after my mother said them to me. I like to re-read them from time to time. They remind me what it is to feel that particular kind of pain—they remind me that loving someone too much gives them the power to destroy you.

my grandfather's hand

my grandfather's hand is cold with death
when I return to his hospital room from dinner—I ordered
La Vie en rose, a gin cocktail, not the song by Edith Piaf
or the sentiment expressed in the words, *to see life through rose-
colored glasses,* which could not have been less applicable, but
I find Edith comforting, her voice nasally, but beautiful, and
I think of her, as I sip my rose-colored drink, with the stacked,
square-shaped ice cubes that hit my face every time I take
a sip—my grandfather is gurgling, he cannot swallow the spit
building in the back of his throat, which they suction up
periodically when I am absent from the room—I keep
coming back to kiss his face as I am trying to leave, afraid
none of the previous kisses were good enough to be the last

Tell Me You're Lying

"You're a monster. I never loved you," I tell him.

It all happens so quickly after that.

He raises a hand and I close my eyes, waiting to feel his palm like a hot iron across my face.

Instead, I hear a crunch and the sound of glass shattering.

There is something cool and hard against my face. I open my eyes. It's the wood floor. I'm lying on the ground. Something warm and wet is dripping into my eyes, blurring my vision.

I try to close them, to surrender to the downward pull, the promise of deep sleep, but he pulls me off the ground by my hair.

"Get up, you stupid bitch," he says. "Look at me."

His eyes are black.

"Take it back," he says.

I smile at him through the pain, all sense of self-preservation vanished. "No," I say.

His face flares and he pushes me backwards. There's another crunch. White, hot pain sears through my feet. I look down. I'm standing in shards of broken glass.

His fingers wrap around my throat. "You're lying."

My body is growing more numb by the minute. Even as he constricts my airway and I can no longer breathe, I don't panic. It's so much easier to surrender. I am so tired of fighting.

"Tell me you're lying," is the last thing I hear before the world goes black.

Greek for: to boil out

I. ἐκ

      your pain
                          organ
bubbles   to the surface
    you bleed
            bewildered
                from the inside

when you sweep the floor

     full of steroids and antihistamines

someone told you it was   anger

     the kind you swallow
           it has to come out somehow

     beautiful body

             you see
the world differently now

     more ghost than person

to be invisible

wake to find the red rash spread across your face

    your heart beats like a hummingbird's

        there is a night that will always haunt you
seeps clear fluid
          to the emergency room
    helpless
            with drugs
    in a cold room wearing

    while a nurse pricks you

      your mother

    touches your arm
you think it's unfair
        this life

    some days
      to take a knife

clean from your bones
        how lovely

II. *ζεῖν*

blotchy red patches
                    you claw them

when you think no one is watching
            your body's ability to burn

    how you shed
            grayish white flakes accumulate

            they want to pump you

                but these are only band aids

                        let grow   inside you

the loss of your soft
            the place you once called home

with a thick kind of bitterness

what you wouldn't give

        the first time
                            you don't eat
            for 3 days
                you feel impossibly light

103

when your face swells
your roommates drive you

sit next to you
as the nurse injects you

paper shirt open in the back

with allergens

you want to tell her to   fuck off

this malfunctioning body
you've been trapped in

you are ready

to strip   the flesh

how satisfying it would be

Essay on Modern Love:
Does it still count if he only tells me he loves me when he's drinking?

I had always thought I would be able to get an abortion, if it wasn't the right time, or with the right person, and I didn't want to trap him into something he didn't want, like his wife had done—even though, of course he *loves* his son, it wasn't the life he chose for himself—but as I stared at the faint—albeit undeniably present—pink line on the pregnancy test, I realized that there is a vast discrepancy between the things you *think* you can do, and the things you can actually do.

He and I met in the psychiatric ward at St. Mary's when I was fifteen. I was visiting my mother, who had tried to kill herself by overdosing on Seroquel the week before. He was this tall, skinny redhead, looking entirely out of place and absolutely miserable in his hospital socks.

I wrote him a note and tucked it into one of the hospital seat cushions. I didn't see him again for almost 2 years, but he was always on my mind. I spent my sophomore year of high school studying abroad in France as a foreign exchange student. We met up when I came home. I was sixteen that summer, and he was turning twenty. We spent an evening at a camp in the woods. That night, he told me I was too young for him.

A couple years later, he impregnated his girlfriend. I graduated from high school in the interim and lived my life away from him— I spent a year at an environmental science school in the middle of nowhere, a year learning how to be a massage therapist, and another year at a hippie school in Boulder, Colorado studying yoga and creative writing, before eventually coming home again. I ran into him in a bar in the fall. He had gained weight and grown a beard. We had sex for the first time that night. I didn't feel the least bit guilty about him having a wife—I was prior.

That winter, I moved out of my aunt's house into my own apartment. He came over drunk a few times in the middle of the night. Months passed like this, and soon it was fall again. He and his wife split up in October, after she discovered he had been having an affair with her maid of honor for over a year.

He sent me a message in January, the night after my grandfather passed away, letting me know he would be there for me if I needed him. I didn't believe him—but now, here we are.

He's decided to be excited about the baby. Last night, he asked me if I was happy, or just happy because he's happy. I asked him what the difference was. He tells me he appreciates me, that no one has ever been so good to him, but he only tells me he loves me when he's drinking.

May 24, 2019

Dear Bill,

J—'s soon to be ex-wife—he filed the divorce papers on Wednesday—is a psychopath. She's been manipulating their son into saying that he wants Mommy and Daddy to get back together . . . He's not even four yet. She's not a good mother. She only had him to trap J— in a relationship with her, and now she's continuing to use him. When he was a baby, one day while J— was at work, she took a nap—because she was so hungover from drinking the night before—and while she was sleeping, he opened the front door of their apartment, and wandered outside into the middle of the heavily trafficked road they lived on, in nothing but a diaper, in the middle of winter.

J— had to hire a lawyer to remove the child endangerment charge from her record, because she was an elementary school teacher at the time, and they won't let you teach children with a charge like that on your record. She didn't last very long as a teacher, though. I guess it's a bit challenging to get up at 6am in the morning and teach a classroom full of little children for 8 hours, when you're habituated to staying up until 2 or 3am drinking. These days she is putting her degree in Early Childhood Education to good use as a bartender.

Yesterday, J— told me she messaged him saying that he didn't have to stay with me just because I'm pregnant. I keep asking myself, *what have I done?* It was never a choice for me, whether or not I would keep the baby. I wanted him from the moment I became aware of the *possibility* of his existence—but sometimes I wonder . . . if I had the opportunity to do it all over, would I have chosen to do things differently? Would I have chosen not to get involved with J— after my grandfather died? If it wasn't for him, I would be an au pair in Italy right now—the plane tickets had already been bought—but instead I'm stuck in Farmington, living with a married man who refuses to tell me how he feels about me. So for all I know, he hates me, but is merely tolerating me, because at least I'm an upgrade from his grossly overweight, lunatic of a wife.

But then I wonder if maybe it was inevitable—unavoidable—as in, I never really had a choice in the first place, so it's useless to ponder that there ever could have, or would have been any other possibility than the one I'm living in right now—if you believe in fate and that sort of thing . . . or maybe nothing has purpose or meaning and we're all just waiting to die.

One last thing before I go—when his wife found out I was pregnant, this is what she said to him—

"I hope she loses it."

Acknowledgements

"Leprechaun," KYSO Flash and Accidents of Light

"How we met," *Catfish Creek*

"Thursdays Are for Therapy," *Miracle Monocle*

"L'amour est aveugle," *Catfish Creek*

"97 Golf," Furrow Magazine

"Manogs," The Halcyone Literary Review and The Sixty-Four: 2018

"Air," KYSO Flash

"Treehouse," Dragon Poet Review

"anxious preoccupied," The Sandy River Review

"to Winter," River and South Review

"désirer," Prairie Margins

"Familiar Face," River and South Review

"my grandfather's hand," *The Mangrove Journal*

"Greek for: to boil out," *The Sandy River Review*

I will be eternally grateful for my creative writing teachers, who gave me their time, insight, and guidance, and without whom the pieces in this collection would not have been publishable. I would specifically like to thank Hattie DeRaps, Gabrielle Lessans, Kurt Gutjahr, Pat O'Donnell, Éireann Lorsung, Jeff Thomson, and especially Bill Mesce, who pushed me to put this collection together, is entirely responsible for its publication, and who believes in my writing in a way I don't think I ever will.

About the Author

Carrie Close was born and raised in Maine, where she lives with her boyfriend Josh, and their two sons, Emerand and Zephyr. You can read more of her work at carrieclose.com.